MEMOIRS OF A BLACK SOUTHERN LAWYER

VOLUME 1

EDWARD BROWN, ESQ.

freedom
LIFE BOOKS

Memoirs of a Black Southern Lawyer

Copyright 2021© Edward Brown, Esq.

Published by Freedom Life Books
P.O. Box 1883
Cypress, Texas 77410
FreedomLifeBooks.com

ISBN: 978-1-953535-20-7

Printed in the United States of America

Memoirs of a Black Southern Lawyer

This memoir covers but one black lawyer's experiences that address a small slice of systemic racism embedded from its inception in this republic called America. The factual settings in this memoir are true. I lived them. Some names of persons, including clients and adversaries, mentioned in this memoir have been changed to protect the innocent and the guilty.

Praise for
Memoirs of a Black Southern Lawyer

"Congratulations for writing this courageous book! Future generations of advocates and lawyers will find this information inspiring as they face similar and new challenges in their careers."

—**Samuel A. Stuckey,**
Retired Senior Level Executive,
INTECOM Corporation

"The authenticity in which this book exposes the real practice of the Uniform Code of Military Justice and the lack of due process when it comes to black servicemembers is spot on. This book should be mandatory reading for all officers in every branch of the military services."

—**Shirley Hill,**
Lt. Col. (Retired Army)

"Mr. Brown has written a brutally honest book based on his personal experiences as a practicing attorney. His book lays bare the racism faced by people of color in our judicial system for 400 plus years. He shows the reader his tenacity on a personal level while representing his clients in a climate of obvious bigotry in the judicial system. Why? Because he lived it. This is a book that every American should read."

—**Attorney Hugh K. Davis**

"In reading this book, I found solace in the fact that Attorney Brown is telling his truths about the underhanded and blatant racism that we have and are still fighting against. He is truly a blessing to individuals such as myself and the many millions of others who he knows and have experienced racism firsthand. THANK YOU! THANK YOU! THANK YOU!"

—**Blondelle C. Gadsden**

Table of Contents

The Preface

There was never a significantly serious and sustained effort by the majority culture to correct the unspeakable wrongs of slavery. That institution, as vile and evil as it was, brought about the economic dominance of America. While some of the early colonists may have had an uneasiness with slavery, there was no manifestation of that in the Constitution. This sinister enterprise and its vestiges have literally destroyed the lives of many millions of Americans. The American judicial system is the functional arm of all levels of Federal, State, city, and county governments that perpetuates the badges of slavery on black people. In rare, although brief interludes, there is a helplessness that I feel as a black man in this country knowing that I cannot bring about any transformational changes to eliminate systemic racism without help from citizens of goodwill from the majority culture. Because of the burden slavery imposes on people who look like me, I sometimes feel guilty in that on multiple occasions I believe I've not done enough to alleviate racism. Power yields nothing without a demand. I feel driven and compelled to always press on for the betterment of the descendants of former slaves.

The racial demographics of America is changing. It is predicted that people of color will constitute the majority of American citizens in twenty to thirty years. There is a school of thought that the recent appointments of ultra conservative Federal Appeals Court and United States District Court Judges by the Trump administration is an attempt to create a judicial apartheid system in this country. Many of these appointees have expressed contempt for racial minorities. As of June 24, 2020, the Trump administration appointed more than forty Appellate Court Judges. None of them are black.

During reconstruction after the Civil War, the original sin of slavery, irretrievably intertwined with the founding of this Republic, could have and should have been fixed. Notwithstanding the 14th and 15th Amendments to the United States Constitution, men of ill will of the confederacy and with the consent from the Union, retrogressed from that era of what could have been. In so doing, states that constituted the former confederate states of America held constitutional conventions between 1880 and 1900 with the pronounce purpose of providing for "*a universal white manhood suffrage and the exclusion from the suffrage of every man with a trace of African blood in his veins.*" An example of this enterprise is what was done in Louisiana. E. B. Kruttschnitt, the President of the Louisiana Constitutional Convention of 1898 proclaimed, "*I say to you that we can appeal to the conscience of the nation, both judicial and legislative and I don't believe that they will take the responsibility of striking down the system we have reared in order to protect the purity of the ballot box and perpetuate the supremacy of the Anglo-Saxon race in Louisiana.*" That functional attitude of supremacy of the White Anglo-Saxon race, predominates, to this day, in the interpretation of laws and regulations, both federal and state, in this country.

CHAPTER 1

Racism—Thomas Jefferson

History provides a basis for understanding the presence of racism in this country. Slavery in America was as American as apple pie. Forty-one out of the fifty-six white men who are commonly referred to as the *"founding fathers"* owned slaves. No serious credibility can be attached to the argument that some of these men were against slavery. James Madison was the author of The Three-fifths Compromise. It is estimated that Jefferson owned about 600 slaves, notwithstanding the fact that he, in the Declaration of Independence, stated that all men are created equal. Obviously, this statement did not apply to slaves. George Washington owned approximately 300 slaves. Madison also owned more than 100 slaves. Madison and his wife hired slaves from adjoining plantation owners to do backbreaking work, but paid the slave owners—and not the slaves—for the forced labor. *Let it be resolved then that those historians who vacillate about this institution have no idea, functional or otherwise, of the degradation, inhumanity, and evilness embedded in slavery.* The Constitution would not have been constructed or ratified without a compromise to enshrine in its bosom the institution of slavery. And for those who assert that it's a myth that the founding fathers supported slavery, I say **they did nothing to**

ban it from the Constitution. The words of my law school torts professor Earl Carl ring so true here, *"If you are not with me, then you are against me."* How dare any in the ivory tower corps of the intelligentsia try unbelievably to convince the descendants of those who were chained like animals, born the physical and mental scars of being unmercifully whipped and treated as chattel, that those white men were against slavery. So, I pose to the reader, what was the ethics or morality of the founding fathers? What manner of man would enslave a fellow human being or approve of a child being ripped away from his parents and sold like livestock to another? I find no hint of basic humanity in any one who condoned those acts. The logical conclusion, then, is that because these people look differently from the founding fathers due to the color of their skin, their freedom could be sacrificed so that the colonies could have a Constitution. Now, some will say some of these white men voiced opposition to the institution of slavery.

On March 15, 1786, John Jay, a founding father, in a letter to R. Lushington, a British judge, said, *"It is much to wish that slavery may be abolished. The honor of the States, as well as justice and humanity, in my opinion, loudly call upon them to emancipate these unhappy people. To contend for our own liberty, and to deny that blessing to others involves an inconsistency not to be excused."* A few others echoed Jay's feelings. But I am attracted to the hypocrisy that John Jay pointed out in his letter. White men were taking up arms demanding their freedom from the British, yet creating a document that would, for almost ninety years, continue to physically enslave black people. I find no morality in hypocrisy.

Codifying slavery in the United States Constitution was the foundation for wealth in this country, particularly in the South. However, it must not be construed that slavery was an institution generated only by Southern **greed.** James DeWolf of Rhode Island is believed by some to be the most prolific slave trader in the history of this country. Historian Keith Stokes estimates that James DeWolf and his family was responsible for bringing (from the shores of Africa) more than 100,000 slaves to this country. The slaves cultivated and harvested cotton in the South. That cotton was then processed in the textile mills in the North. DeWolf was heavily invested in the mills. By the time of his death in 1837, James DeWolf was the second richest man in America. Slavery became the linchpin in the American economic engine.

In the same vein, but on another (more vile) level, that engine could not be fueled without the well-orchestrated efforts from men like Edward Rutledge. Rutledge was one of the signers of the Declaration of Independence. He, along with Arthur Middleton and Thomas Heyward, Jr., represented South Carolina in regards to the final wording of the Declaration of Independence. Their efforts, together with representatives Button Gwinett, Lyman Hall, and George Walton from Georgia, were principally responsible for any anti-slavery language not being in the Declaration of Independence. Slavery was an American enterprise. With this free labor, America rose to an economic power. So then, none should seriously debate that the canonizing of slavery into the fabric of the American judicial system was put in place to support the American economy.

Religious institutions in the colonies bore an equal responsibility in the ratification of slavery. Many churches and priests, like the Anglicans, owned slaves. How two-faced were these religious leaders? They left England to escape religious persecution but sanctioned one human being owned as property by another. I'm reminded of a conversation with one of my Nigerian college mates, Francis Obgula, in which he said the following, *"When the missionaries came to Africa, they had the Bible and my ancestors had the land. The missionaries said to them, let us kneel and pray. When my ancestors got up from praying, the missionaries had the land and we had the Bible."*

The primary author of the Declaration of Independence was Thomas Jefferson. Jefferson was a lawyer, plantation owner, and scientist. Twenty-two of the fifty-six original signers of the Declaration of Independence were lawyers. If there was any appetite to make the Declaration of Independence applicable to all human beings in the American colonies, there were certainly enough lawyers present to make that thought clear. The United States Constitution was adopted on September 17, 1787, some ten years after the signing of the Declaration of Independence. History has recorded no event that would lead me to conclude that these white men engaged in any significant efforts to illustrate that the words in the Declaration of Independence, *"We hold these truths to be self-evident, that all men are created equal, that they are endowed by their Creator or with certain unalienable rights, that among these are life, liberty and the pursuit of happiness,"* applied to black people. Could it be that the Declaration of Independence's principal author believed black people had a different creator?

Some historians have referred to Jefferson as the most transformative figure in early American history. For the most part, I would agree with those historians. For, Jefferson was reflective of the most domineering intellectual thoughts of the time.

Jefferson made very clear notes that reflected his ideas about slavery. Jefferson, in those notes, says, *"beside those of color, figure, and hair, there are other physical distinction(s) proving a different of race. They have less hair on their face and body.*

They secrete less by the kidneys and more by the glands of their skin, which give them very strong and disagreeable odor. This greater degree of transpiration renders them more tolerant of heat, and less so of cold, than whites. Perhaps to a different of structure in the pulmonary apparatus, which a late ingenuous experimental list has discovered to be the principal regulator of animal heat, may have been disabled them from extricating, in the act of inspiration, so much of that fluid from the outer air, or oblige them in expiration, to point with more of it. They seem to require less sleep. All black(s), after hard labor through the day, will be induced by the slightest amusements to sit up till midnight, or later, though knowing he must be up with the first dawn on the morning. They are least as brave and more adventuresome. But this may perhaps proceed from a want of forethought, which prevents their seeing a danger to it be present. When present, they do not go through it with more coolness or steadiness than the whites. They are more ardent after their females, but love seems with them to be more an eager desire, then a tender delicate mixture of sentiment and sensation. Their griefs are transient. . . In general, their existence appears to participate more of sensation than reflection. Comparing them by their faculties of memory, reason, and imagination, it appears to me, that in memory they are equal to whites; in reason much inferior, as I think one could scarcely be found capable of tracing and comprehending the investigations of Euclid; and that in imagination they are dull, tasteless, and anomalous."

The heartfelt view of Jefferson captured in his notes, can be used as a template for a manifesto of any 20th Century white supremacist group. Jefferson argued, through his writings, that because of the color of their skin, Caucasians are naturally superior to Africans. He made no distinction between males and females. Yet, having these vicious views of blacks as being inferior, he nonetheless first impregnated

Sally Hemings, an African-American female, when she was a mere child at the tender age of fifteen. Rhetorically, I ask, *What morally guided man would impregnate a fourteen-year-old child?* Many ill guided historians, in order to perpetuate the myth of this pristine white man, not possibly having fathered children with Sally Hemings, constructed elaborate explanations in attempts to prove that this scoundrel had not fathered any children with Ms. Hemings. However, all of those historians' conclusions were swept aside to their rightful position, on the trash heap of false history, when DNA definitively proved that Jefferson was the father of Sally Hemings' children.

I have never been able to understand how the Europeans could **invade** this continent, systematically murder the Native Americans, and enslave Africans in America when they left Europe to escape oppression. Jefferson's disposition and attitude towards non-Caucasians set the tone for the foundation upon which America is built. That foundation is still intact. Yes, the country has made strides toward a more perfect union. However, many lives have been lost and destroyed, dreams deferred, and human dignity taken away from those who do not look like the dominant class. Sometimes, I am overcome with this never-ending grind to secure equality for all Americans.

CHAPTER 2

First Encountering Racism

As I composed my memoirs, I would sit on the back porch, sometimes in temperature with a heat index of 110 degrees. I was asked "why?". As I thought of my ancestors having to work in the slave owners' fields from sunup to sundown in unimaginably hot, squalid and inhumane conditions, there is a contemplation that perhaps cerebrally I could manifest a re-creation of what they had to contend with. My attempt at replication is feeble at best. But from that analysis, I draw a strength which catapults me forward to let all who read these words know there is a story to tell, untethered to any concept, except for the truth. The truth is not always pleasant, but it should be unrelentingly told. By putting pen to paper, it is not my intent to offend anyone. But I am sure some will be offended. When I was growing up as a little boy, my family had a hog pen with numerous pigs in the enclosure. I would throw rocks at the animals and only the critter that the rock struck would squeal. It is my fervent hope that only those who are struck by these words will yell.

My first conscious memory of racism occurred when I was a young lad at a livestock auction with my father. Every year he would take two or three cows and some hogs to sell in Walterboro, South Carolina. The animals that we brought to be sold had not yet been run through the chute into an open pen so that they could be viewed by people in attendance. The auctioneer went on break for lunch and my father said that we were going to get something to eat. We didn't go far. We walked to a little restaurant very near to where the auction was being held. As he grabbed my hand, he directed us to the back door. I thought that was rather strange because the white people were going in the front door of the restaurant and could sit down at a table to eat. I asked my father why we couldn't go through the front door of the restaurant and sit down to eat at the table like the white men. His response was, *"The buckras don't want to sit and eat with Negroes."* Further confusing my own mind, was the fact that there was a little open window with the shelf protruding out at the back of the restaurant. I only saw black people standing in line waiting to have their food orders taken. There was no place to sit down to eat the food. As did all of the others before us in the line, and I presume all of those behind us, my father and I got our orders in a little brown bag and walked back to the truck that he drove to bring the livestock to Walterboro so that we could sit down and eat.

I thought it was so unfair that we had to eat in our truck and weren't allowed to come through the front door while the white men sat and ate at tables in the restaurant. I didn't quite understand the term *"buckra,"* but would later on equate the term with being Caucasian.

During the drive back from Walterboro to Wadmalaw Island, I wanted to further ask my father about why we couldn't sit in the restaurant to eat our food. However, knowing him, as I did, being a man of few words, I feared posing any question to him about what we, as well as the other Black people, had just experienced. I have very little memory, if any, of the other things he talked to me about during the drive back. I just remember thinking that this man, as tough as he was, was my hero and yet he had to humble himself, by way of going to the back of the restaurant to secure food to eat. Maybe that is when the idea first lodged itself in my soul that I would try to do something to fundamentally change what occurred to my father and the other Black people on that day in Walterboro, South Carolina.

That is not to be construed as a representation that all white people are evil. To say that, it would be a categorical lie. What I observed was a subservient relationship between most whites and blacks. For the most part, there was very little socialization between the two races, except on an employer/employee basis. Most of the black people on Wadmalaw Island that did not have jobs in the nearest city, Charleston, South Carolina, worked for white-owned farmers as field hands. That was not true for me, my siblings, and nephews. Our father and my nephew's grandfather, had a farm of approximately twenty-five acres. As a footnote, none of that came from the forty acres and a mule that was promised to most black people after the Civil War. Frank Brown strictly forbade us from working on any white man's farm.

But in the summertime, he would haul potatoes for some of the major farmers to the packing shed to be processed. That work, which lasted about two weeks, would be done by his children and grandchildren. The money earned from that enterprise was used, in part, to finance the purchase of school clothing for the upcoming school year, which began in August, for the children and grandchildren. For the rest of the summer, we would be required to harvest the crops from our farm. We planted corn, cabbage, squash, cucumber, snap beans, watermelons, and collard greens.

The farming almost exclusively was done by my parents, their children and grandchildren. We ranged in ages from seven to eighteen. There were seven boys and two girls who lived in the house during these years. He had, that is my father had, a day job. In the mornings, before going to work, he would set out assignments that must be performed by all of the children and grandchildren for that day. If any work was not completed, everyone would be punished. While we didn't understand why all had to suffer if one did not complete the work that was assigned, it later became clear that he was creating a dynamic that instilled in us the concept that we must help and be responsible for each other. That basic principle remains a part of my family to this day.

During those formative years, I was always envious of the friends and schoolmates that went to New York and other northern cities to visit relatives for the summer. While they were away experiencing life, inasmuch as they could, in places like Philadelphia, Washington, DC, and Chicago, me, my siblings, and nephews labored in the hot sun cultivating the various vegetables on the farm. During the summer, the days would begin around 7:00 a.m. but no later than 8:00 a.m. The work would continue until 12:00 p.m. You were allowed to take an hour for lunch and sit under a shaded tree for some much-needed rest. Most of the time, my mother would have prepared lunch for the children working in the fields. One person was always assigned to go get the lunch from our house and bring it to where the work was occurring. When everyone was ushered to the fields in a vehicle driven by one of the older children, on rare occasions lunch would consist of a honey bun and a Pepsi, purchased from Ted's store.

During the good years when my father anticipated that the prices for the vegetables to be taken to the market would be elevated, he would rent additional acreage to plant truck crops and vegetables. That necessarily meant more work for me, my nephews and siblings during the planting and harvesting seasons. In those good years, although there were not many, he would hire other children our age from the community to help with mostly harvesting, and in some cases, during the planting season. As I reflect back on those springs and summers on the farm, I am now forever grateful that my parents did not let us go north to stay with relatives during the summer. The work was hard, the sun was hot, and the days long. But we never quit until the assignments that were given in the morning were completed.

While I did not realize then what was being taught to us by my parents, the hard work and completion of tasks instilled a work ethic that permeates me and my siblings and grandchildren. Because of that work principal, my motto has been during my professional life, that while I may not win all of the cases that I take on, I will not lose any because I am out worked by my opponent. That desire was buttressed by one of my law school professors. He, an intellectual giant, informed me that if your opponent, (who's probably going to be white), reads twenty cases in preparation for his argument, you must read forty because you will have to be twice as good as your opponent and educate the judge, (who is almost always white), on what the law is and how it has been interpreted through the case law just to, perhaps, get a fair shake.

CHAPTER 3

High School Years and Racism

Some ten years after the Supreme Court's decision in *Brown v. Board of Education*, the State of South Carolina came up with the plan to integrate its school under a statutory enactment allowing for *"freedom of choice."* In the tenth grade, as I understood the plan, it meant that the students and their parents had the choice to attend any school in the school district. Before this *"freedom of choice"* plan came into vogue with the State of South Carolina, I went to all-black Haut Gap High School. The all-white high school was St. John's. Both schools were located on Johns Island, South Carolina, less than a mile from each other. I can't quite remember how I ever envisioned that I wanted to be one of the first black students to go to the all-white St. John's High School. Maybe it was a desire to be one of the first or maybe it was pure ignorance. However, after discussing the matter with my father, he agreed to allow me to attend St. John's High School at the beginning of my junior year in 1965. My mother died two years earlier. If she was still alive, perhaps she would have argued against me embarking on the whim to become a student at St. John's High School.

Nothing in my freshman and sophomore years and Haut Gap High School prepared me for the mental assaults that occurred on a daily basis at St. John's High School. Although we had secondhand books at Haut Gap, the environment was nurturing and the teachers cared very deeply about their students learning and succeeding. One teacher in particular, Rosemound Gilliard, was a most profound educator. She instilled in me, and many others, a burning desire to be the best. Her teaching style, demeanor, and entire persona conveyed the notion that no matter the obstacles, failure was not in our future.

Whatever notions I possessed at that time, of being treated fairly by the majority of white students, teachers and administrators at St. John's High School, were brutally ended after the first day at school. And I must say that it is not that I did not know that racism existed, for I did. I was aware, through the news media, of attempts to integrate various institutions in American society. However, none of those efforts involved me personally, therefore I had no firsthand knowledge of what it meant or how these Black Americans were feeling internally when they were spat on, called *"nigger"* or *"coon."* Upon reflection, maybe it was benign ignorance.

When confronted with this kind of racist behavior, I was sometimes overwhelmed by the ferocity and viciousness embedded in and exhibited by students, teachers, and a super majority of the administrators. Every morning at the bus stop, it was a profound struggle for me to summon up the courage to withstand the brutalness of the coming day. Without fail, the reprehensible conduct began when I got on the bus. I was later told by a prominent black clergyman, Rev. Leon Bolton, that law enforcement actually followed the buses, on a daily basis, that I and other black students boarded to get to and from St. John's High School. From the time I got on the bus, my focus was to survive the rest of the day without incurring any mental or physical damage from white students, teachers, and administrators.

Most of my teachers, during my junior year, were extremely savage in their comments and conduct towards me and all other black students. One teacher in particular, was an unabashed racist. Ms. Grant would allow and indeed encourage white students to refer to the black students as *"niggers," "jungle bunnies," "coons,"* etc. I was the only black student in the history class that she taught. One day, a white student came by my desk and dropped a banana peel on it. Ms. Grant laughed, along with the other students. I had to create in my mind a pillow, a crutch, on which to lean to sustain myself during those daily barrages levied against me solely because of the color of my skin. One of those crutches in which I found solace, was the mental framework of comparing this teacher's look to that of a turtle. Her cleavage was down to her knees and her behind was as flat as a board. Her facial features were such that a turtle was pretty compared to her. I thought, how could someone whose looks were so unpleasing to the eyes be disparaging toward me? I remember once remarking to one of my African-American schoolmates that this teacher looked so ugly that she gave ugly a bad name. While some may criticize my description of this teacher, at that time, I had to do everything I could to maintain my sanity and strength to survive this vile situation.

Most of the pop quizzes and/or exams did not lend themselves to subjective grading. I did well on objective exams. I believe to this day, that if this teacher had her druthers, she would have given me a failing grade.

The white male students were the most offensive culprits. None of them would confront you for the purposes of engaging in fisticuffs by themselves. I was somewhat muscular and tried to present an aura that if you attacked me, much and possibly fatal harm would be delivered to you. Most of the time, the confrontations would occur when it was many of them and a few of us. The physical threat was such that the African-American male students would be together at lunch so as to prevent isolated gang attacks. As far as I can remember, there were no physical attacks during classes by white male students against African-American students. However, if an attack were going to occur, it would be during recess in a setting where the gang could isolate a single African-American student. At no time during my two years at St. John's High School were there more than ten African-American male students enrolled. We came up with a plan to never be isolated from one another during the recess period. That meant that we would eat together, go to the bathroom together, and migrate about the school grounds as a group.

One day I had just left geometry class to go to lunch. On this frightful day, I, along with four other African-American male students, went to the restroom. We were all in various stages of completing our business with the latrine when through the door came about ten gruesome white boys. The leader of the group was John Eddy. He later became a South Carolina Highway patrolman. I, along with my fellow warriors, proceeded to a posture designed to inflict maximum physical harm on the attackers. I instinctively took off my belt and wrapped it around my left-hand knuckle with the buckle in a position to cause the most pain when used to strike a blow to the aggressors. In my right-hand, I placed a compass with the sharpest point firmly entrenched between the thumb and index finger, and tightly gripped by the remaining fingers on my hand. I thought that we would take a beating, but I was going to cause as many injuries as I could to one or more of these assailants. Just as these assailants began to move towards us, the bathroom door swung open and in came the assistant principal, Mr. Jones. He admonished, only verbally, the assaulters by way of telling them to leave the bathroom immediately. With some reluctance, they did.

I was never more pleased to see a white man as I was on that day. While I believe that we would have given a good account of ourselves in the combat, we probably would have received some severe injuries also.

Because the daily threat of physical violence was always present, I sat at the back of the classroom. My thoughts were that I would have a better opportunity to see and analyze whatever mischief was being contemplated by the white students, and in some instances, the teacher as it related to me.

One particular occasion occurred with a white male student by the name of Mike Lorton. Lorton was probably 5'7" in height and very stocky. Fat on his frame was nowhere to be found. As we were about to change classes, he, along with two of his minions, approached me in the classroom. Both of us were standing. Lorton was right in my face. His two companions were about two to three feet behind him on either side. He took a paperback novel that was about three quarters of an inch thick and literally tore it in half. That act was done to scare me. Truth be told, I was frightened to my core. But, I could not and would not show outwardly, my inner feelings. Our eyes interlocked. I stared him in the face so as to say bring it on. I took less than one-half step backwards. My purpose was to be positioned such that I could deliver a crushing right-hand blow to his face. I thought that was all that I would be able to do because I was outnumbered three to one. This situation had all the trappings to become very ugly for me. All of the other white students stayed to see this possible beatdown. Lorton was performing for his audience.

On the other hand, if I took out the leader with one punch then perhaps the two others would think twice about carrying the attack forward. If Lorton had made even the slightest move towards me that I thought was aggressive, my right hand, with a closed fist, would be unleashed to his head. He made no such move. Realizing from my demeanor and posture that I was prepared to do battle with him, he backed down and his comrades followed his lead. I will confess to the world that I was happy as happy could be.

Interestingly, before this confrontation occurred, the teacher left the classroom with about five minutes left in the period. That teacher never left the class early prior to that. Nor did she leave early again after the incident. To this day, I am convinced that the teacher knew what was about to occur between me and those three white male students.

The mental stress associated with being constantly bombarded with racial epithets was the worst. And none of the white teachers, except for one or two would do anything to stop the conduct. During the school day, there was no refuge, no oasis on which a fifteen-to-sixteen-year-old could seek relief from the mental hell and possible physical attacks. There would be discussions and discourse among the black students about how to best handle the hateful situation. All of us were struggling with this abrasive and hostile atmosphere at St. John's. There was no need to take our complaints to the principal, Mr. Higgins. He was just as racist as the super majority of the administrative staff. There were approximately fifteen to twenty black students who transferred to St. John's High School in the fall of 1966. None of us, as I recall, were in the same classes during that year except for homeroom.

While I craved for another black face in any of my classes during the course of the day, that was not to be. I believe it was a conscious effort of the school administration to isolate us from each other in the classroom. During recess we would share horror stories of what was done to us in class during the previous periods. I surmised that the plan of the principal and those in cahoots with him was to bombard each individual black student with racial epithets, among other things, during the class. Their purpose was to make as many of the black students that came over in the fall of 1966 leave St. John's High School that same year. After a two-week period, more than half of the African-American students left St. John's High School to return to the school from which they came.

However, I do believe the assistant principal, Mr. Jones, was the most sympathetic administrator to the plight of the black students. But even he could not and did not shield us from the perpetual racist verbal onslaught perpetrated by the white students.

Separate and apart from the constant racial epithets and harassment, I still had to make good grades. I specifically remember geometry class. The teacher Ms. Williamson, would give extra credit for questions that were answered over and above the ten questions that usually comprised the exam. At the end of the semester, a white student had a higher average, although my exam grades were higher than his. I would always answer the extra questions. That experience coupled with others, propelled me to believe that most of the teachers in my junior year were not going to allow a black student to have the highest grade in any class at the end of the semester or school year.

I looked forward to going to the prom my junior year. That thought was as naïve as any I have ever had in my life.

Although St. John's did have a prom all the years before the black students arrived, they were not going to allow us to be at a school-sponsored prom with the white students. The principal officially cancelled the school prom. The white students and administrators had an off-campus prom instead. You could only attend if you are invited. Needless to say, the prom remained all-white, for no blacks were invited. The same nonsense continued during our senior year. I was deprived of ever going to a high school prom, solely because I was black.

The guidance counselor at St. John's High School was a Caucasian female that had a deep-seated aversion to black students in general and black males in particular. I vividly remember, during my senior year, having to meet with the guidance counselor for the purpose of making preparations to attend college. This woman was overtly racist. Frankly, because of prior encounters with her, I was very hesitant to try to secure any help from her for any reason. However, being a sixteen-year-old trying to get ready to go to college, I needed any help I could in making that happen.

On the day of our meeting, in her office, she gave this aura that was contemptuous in nature, so as to suggest, "Why are you, *black son-of-a-bitch*, in my office?" Because she was the guidance counselor and I was a student, as uncomfortable as it was, I had to go through the process. I remember specifically, she asked the question, "What is it that you want to do after you graduate?" My response was, "I want to be an aeronautical engineer or a lawyer." The look on her face was one of bitter disgust. Her face then turned red. I understood enough to know that my answer to her question was upsetting to her. It was as if she thought that I should have answered the question dramatically different.

That moment, given the look on her face, has forever been etched in my memory. She proceeded to tell me a number of reasons why she thought my career goals were not realistic and doomed for failure. All the while, I never saw her look at any files that she may have had on her desk or any grades that constituted my performance at St. John's High School. She finally told me that she did not think I was college material and that I would do better in the arts and crafts.

For the average sixteen-year-old, that kind of assessment of one's abilities by the school guidance counselor would be crushing. But I thank God every day for Frank and Hattie Brown being my parents. They instilled in me and my siblings, the unshakable belief that "no one is better than you and you can do anything that you want to if you work hard." I simply refused to allow this woman to penetrate the armor in which my dreams were sheltered. This white woman, I decided, was not going to throw me off-track.

This was one of the many days during my monumentally stressful junior and senior years at St. John's High School that I relied on the words of Ms. Gilliard, to carry me through to the final bell of the day. As I reflect on the possible ramifications of that day, I ponder how many black children are pummeled with this notion of not being able to achieve their goals by white authoritative figures in the school system because they are deemed not academically capable.

At that point, I thought that it would be indeed, a pleasure for me to pay a visit to her after I graduated from college or law school. Unfortunately, she died a very hard death before I could show her my degree from the University of California at Berkeley. She robbed me of that pleasure.

CHAPTER 4

Two Years at St. John's High School and Football Tryout

Some who read this memoir will conclude that this writer has an aversion for white people. One of the simple models that guides my existence on this earth is to treat others as you want to be treated. I have no hatred for anyone because of the color of their skin. During those torturous two years at St. John's High School, I can and will say without equivocation, that there was one teacher who exhibited fairness to me and other African-American students. I suspect that she probably caught hell from some of her fellow teachers because she did not engage in the racially motivated venom towards black students that was the daily and constant for the other white educators. She taught French, and I believe having lived abroad in France, her attitude towards the black students was much more even handed. Also, Ms. Searson, who was just a very decent human being, from my viewpoint, did not let the race of students guide her conduct towards the black children. As much as she could, Ms. Searson tried to render comfort, psychologically, to me and other blacks whom she taught. Other than her, I have no recollection of any other white teacher being fair and even handed to me and others who look like me during our horrid years at St. John's High School.

On the opposite end of the spectrum was the football coach, a man named White. At the beginning of my senior year, I approached White about playing football. He was very blunt and unapologetic in his response. He said, *"We're not letting any niggers play this year."* Should I have been crushed? Yes. Was I? No. The previous year left me with no delusions about the difficulties I and the black students would encounter from most of those white teachers, administrators, and coaches until we graduated. The year after I graduated, one of my friends was actually allowed to participate in football practice by White. There was a drill that White developed simply for the purpose of convincing Harry that he would not be able to play. The three on one drill put Harry, who probably weighed 150 pounds with a couple of bricks in his back pocket, against three mammoth white offensive linemen. This drill would be conducted while every other member of the football team looked on. Sometimes it would go on for as much as thirty minutes. Every five to ten minutes, there would be a substitution of the white offensive lineman to pound on Harry. After about three days of this madness, Harry turned in his football equipment and never returned to practice. That was the result that White and the other white coaching staff wanted.

I sense, every now and then, that a few of the white students, especially girls, wanted to be friendly. But integration was a new thing for them and for us. It was akin to a herd mentality that permeated all, but a very few, of the white students. The verbal attacks with racial epithets; visceral locutions about how we smelled, looked, and talked, were constant. This kind of conduct was exhibited even in the classroom, sometimes, and most of the teachers would do nothing to admonish the student or students. However, these acts of racism were most vicious during recess. Some of the white students gathered in groups and it appeared as if they were competing to determine who could make the most vile comment. Now, it is not to be construed that every white student participated in this horrendous phenomenon. For there were some who did not. And at this stage of my existence, I don't blame those few for not standing up and telling their peers that they were being mean to the black students or that they should not make the kind of vicious racist remarks that were common occurrences. For to do so would have probably resulted in those students being ostracized by the groups that were leading the racial stereotyping against black students.

Very few, if any, of the black students, including myself, took a passive, verbally nonviolent approach in responding to these hateful comments. My favorite comeback to most of the verbal barrage that included the word *"nigger"* was *"your momma is a nigger."* Other than giving me some momentary solace, that retort didn't have the effect that I believed it would. In the black community, at least when I was growing up, to talk about someone's mother in a derogatory manner was fighting words. In my mind, I was baiting the opponent, especially male white students, into physical confrontations. No one ever took the bait. I was 6'1" tall with the weight of about 195 pounds. There was no flab on my frame. I thought maybe none of the male students took the bait because of my physique. I later came to understand that my telling one of them that *"your mama is a nigger,"* did not resonate as it would with most black people. I never feared any of the white male students could subdue me in a one-on-one physical altercation. In that regard, all of the black students, especially male, surmised that any one of us would be heavily disadvantaged in a situation where a gang of white males were to attack a single individual. I never had any desire to confront a white female in a combative situation.

We are all products of and molded by our environments. In my professional life, the approach I took in practicing law was predicated upon, in large part, those two years at St. John's High School. Every day, as a black lawyer I had to get up and prove myself anew. It mattered not how much success I had the previous day or days, for you were always judged by the professional skills and intellect that you exhibited in the moment. God forbid that you would make a mistake. It is analogous to a theory that has evolved about playing golf. Take no consolation in the spectacular shot you just hit, concentrate only on the shot that you are about to take.

Notwithstanding the fact that you are human accompanied by frailties, you could never make an error without being severely scrutinized and deemed professionally incompetent. My white counterparts were never saddled with such a burden in their practice of law. It was a common cliché among black lawyers that some clients could be told by a white lawyer that two plus two is five and they would believe it just because the lawyer was white. If we, as black lawyers, said that two plus two was four, sometimes our client (even if he or she were black) wouldn't believe it. Here again, the ugly phenomenon of self-hatred raised its head.

CHAPTER 5

The Medical Vestiges of Slavery

In growing up on Wadmalaw Island, there were not many emotionally useful encounters that I had with white people. The house my parents lived in was about 100 yards from a four-way traffic intersection at Bears Bluff, Harts Bluff, and Liberia Road. One day, some neighborhood kids and I were playing in our yard. We heard the sounds of two automobiles colliding. Immediately, I realized that the collision occurred at the four-way intersection. There had been automobile accidents there before. Our curiosity heightened and we ran to the scene of the accident. One car was in the middle of the intersection. This vehicle and the passenger inside who had suffered the most severe damages were pointed in a catty-corner direction in the intersection. The passenger in the car, Mrs. Mack, was significantly injured. She was a very robust black woman who was a mother of eight. She was revered in the black community as a church-going Christian person. Her husband, who was the driver of the car, and some other adults had already removed her from the car by the time my playmates and I arrived. Mrs. Mack was in obvious pain laying on the side of the road. Visually, I could tell that her left leg was severely injured. I believe it was broken.

A white doctor by the name of Pettis lived off of Harts Bluff Road. Pettis was on his way home from work. In order to get to his house, he had to drive through the intersection where the collision occurred. To his credit, he stopped at the scene of the accident, but he did nothing else. He gave a scornful look at Mrs. Mack, who was in obvious and excruciating discomfort, lying on the ground. In her groaning, it was as if she was saying to Dr. Pettis, *please help me*. He did nothing, said nothing, and looked at her with disdain, so as to convey the message, you are below me as a human being and I, despite my medical training, will do nothing to aid you during your discomfort. To that point in my short time on this earth, that contemptible glare was the most vile conduct that I had witnessed one human being exhibiting towards another. That memory has plagued me every day of my earthly existence. At that tender age, it became clear that some white people believe that they are superior in all rims of life to persons who do not have the hue of their epidermis.

He left the accident scene and went home without uttering a word to Mr. or Mrs. Mack. I remember thinking, "She was badly injured with tears coming from her eyes and he rendered no assistance, not even a word to comfort her in the distressful situation." I asked myself, "Why would he not provide any aid to Mrs. Mack?"

Later on, after I started practicing law, I understood better the conduct of Dr. Pettis and the dreadful way he treated Mrs. Mack. He was one of the most notable physicians at Roper Hospital in Charleston, South Carolina. Dr. Pettis was on the Board of Commission of Roper Hospital for nineteen years. He was Chairman of the Board eight of those years. Roper Hospital was completely segregated, and I do mean completely. It only became integrated after it was ordered by the Federal Court in 1969. In its opinion, the court noted, "Roper Hospital has been and is regarded in the Charleston community, and particularly among Negroes, as a white-only hospital." The court order also quoted a part of a news article from the local newspaper, *The News and Courier*. The article read in part, "In March 1965, Roper announced it would discontinue programs under the Department of Health Education and Welfare following the passage of the 1964 Civil Rights Act." In other words, Roper chose to discontinue receiving federal funds rather than integrate its facility. In 1965, the court order stated:

> "following the enactment of Title VI of the Civil Rights Act of 1964, prohibiting federal financial assistance to recipients, including hospitals, which fail to comply with federal desegregation requirements, the doctor who was then Chief of Roper's medical staff brought before the Society a motion to sign a compliance agreement pursuant to the Civil Rights Act of 1964…The motion was defeated on the stated grounds that the members felt that federal aid would ultimately lead to interference with the Roper Hospital policy. Roper Hospital also discontinued its participation in all federal programs."

While I have no firsthand knowledge as to whether Dr. Pettis voted for or against the agreement, I believe with certainty, that given how he looked at, and failed to administer any aid to Ms. Mack on that dreadful day, with a rational basis I can infer that he voted against the agreement with the United States Government.

When the automobile collision that severely injured Ms. Mack occurred, I was in the third grade. Sixty years later,

I am aware of very little conduct on the part of Roper Hospital that leads me to conclude that they have progressed much beyond the mindset of Dr. Pettis or the members of the Board of Directors that voted in 1965 to discontinue receiving federal funds rather than integrate the facility.

In July 2015, I filed a lawsuit in the United States District Court for the District of South Carolina against Roper Hospital and several of its white doctors on the leadership team, on behalf of a black doctor. My client was immaculately qualified. He had graduated in the upper ten percent of his class from the University of North Carolina Medical School. His road to becoming a doctor was not easy. He, much more so than I, came from very, very, humble beginnings. At one point during his childhood, he was homeless. In spite of very hard times growing up, Dr. Robinson was determined to be a physician and had the intellect to accomplish that goal.

He was hired by Roper Hospital with a plethora of promises made by Roper to entice him to sign a contract. At the time he was hired, he was the only African-American, of sixty physicians, that practiced at that Roper Hospital location. Overall, Roper Hospital had only seven black physicians on its staff of approximately 200 doctors. It became excruciatingly clear to Dr. Robinson that Roper did not want him to succeed. He was, on most all occasions, never given an adequate space in which to practice or render professional care to patients. That was not true for any of the Caucasian doctors. After seeing patients, Dr. Robinson had to stand up at a counter to record the chart notes regarding their visits. The white doctors were given office space, clerical help, and other support services. Dr. Robinson was not provided with any of those accommodations. Yet, he was expected to treat as many patients as the white doctors although he did not have an office in which to accomplish that undertaking. Many days his white counterparts were not using their offices to see patients. However, Dr. Robinson was not allowed to use the white doctors' empty offices to treat his patients. I thought that was ludicrous. The more Dr. Robinson complained about his lack of support, the worse the treatment became. Roper's discriminatory history against black patients and doctors has not subsided. It is still being practiced in a most robust fashion.

Early on in my representation of Dr. Robinson, it became clear to me that the situation that Roper Hospital had put him in was designed to get him to quit or lose his privilege to practice medicine. The practice of medicine is stressful enough. His state of affairs with Roper was hellish at best. His crisis attracted the attention of the same newspaper that had reported, some fifty years before, that Roper would cut all financial ties with the federal government rather than integrate its facilities. Dr. Robinson had every right to make the public aware of his plight at the hands of Roper Hospital. The story of his treatment, because of his race, was told in *The News and Courier* for all to read. For me, there was no rational reason that could be given for the treatment he received from Roper Hospital other than being black. What was baffling to me was that individual white doctors who were named as defendants in this lawsuit were incensed that they were accused of discriminating against my client. It was as though they expected to routinely engage in discriminatory acts against my client and he was supposed to like it, apparently. This attitude of *how dare you accuse me of discriminating against you, although I am*, gave me the distinct impression that these white doctors thought my client was supposed to let them kick him in his ass without complaining.

After filing the lawsuit, Roper's outside counsel requested, on three separate occasions, an extension of time in which to file their answer. I found him to be a very forthright and decent person. Although he was twenty years my junior, I was significantly impressed with his lawyering skills. I graciously consented to each request, but my client had made me aware that Roper Hospital was competing with Medical University of South Carolina to become the primary health care provider of Boeing Aircraft Company. Boeing was one of the biggest employers in this area. Boeing's workforce was approximately thirty-eight percent black. I did not think, in my calculations, that a contract between Boeing and Roper would be finalized without Dr. Robinson's case being settled. It would have been a public relations disaster for Boeing to sign a contract with Roper to be the primary healthcare provider for the local workforce if there was a race discrimination lawsuit brought by an African-American physician being litigated in the courts.

Sometimes one's path through life intersects with the events in history over which he has no control. Tragically, the white supremacist, Dylan Roof, thirty days earlier on June 17, 2015, entered Emanuel AME Church in Charleston, South Carolina, and murdered nine black parishioners during Bible study. While both my client and I were saddened by that horrific crime, we pressed on to vindicate Dr. Robinson's claims.

This contract with Boeing would mean Roper Hospital would reap many millions of dollars in income. Further, because lawsuits are a matter of public record, I firmly believe that Roper Hospital did not want any record of having denied, in a court proceeding, that discrimination occurred at their institution. Mediation can occur anytime, even before pleadings are filed in the federal courts. I am convinced that the best way they thought to conclude this matter without the fear of publicity, would be through mediation. Never before in my, at that time, thirty-eight years of practice, had I been approached by an opponent in a lawsuit to mediate the case without an Answer being filed. When a Plaintiff files a summons and complaint in any court proceeding, the rules require that the defendant files a response to the allegations in the plaintiff's complaint within a specified time frame. Because I was so used to employment discrimination cases being drawn out and la-bor-intensive, I was unsure what to make of this offer to me-diate. Somewhat timid as I was, I believe that my client and I had the better hand in this game. I prepared for mediation as though I was going to try the case before a jury in open court.

One of the tactics that I always use in mediation is after about two to three hours, I inform the mediator that the other side is BS*ing* and my client and I are preparing to leave. That lets me know if the opposing counsel seriously wants to con-clude the case through mediation. If the mediator comes back to us after delivering my rant to the opposing side, saying that they have put more money on the table so don't leave yet, my client and I know we are now in the controlling position with the advantage. The only question for the rest of the mediation is how much money will the case be settled for. It could not have worked better in this case. Roper knew that we knew that the potential contract with Boeing was worth many, many, millions of dollars. They were not going to allow this case to blow up that contract. This time my calculations were spot on. After about eight hours of mediation, with a good media-tor, a settlement was reached. This took place fifty-seven days after the case was filed in the United States District Court. Never before did I know of any employment discrimination case concluded that expeditiously. Both my client and I were happy with the monetary figure.

CHAPTER 6

Orange Memorial Hospital

W hen my friends would return from their summer vaca-
tions in the North, there would be a number of stories
about not having to use *"black only"* water fountains and
restrooms after they passed the Mason-Dixon Line. There was
the constant exaltation by my oldest sister and other relatives of
how great it was to live and work in New York and the north.
The many stories I heard about the good living by blacks in that
region of the country created in my mind a distinct belief that
there was very little, if any, race discrimination in the north.
While at age ten I considered myself well-read from the secondhand textbooks the white children used the year before, there
was very little classroom discussions about racism in the North
to confirm or deny my beliefs. I knew first-hand about racial
discrimination in the South because I lived with it every day. We
had no occasion to read books about the vicious and brutal incidents of racial violence, such as the New York City draft riots,
nor did we learn that Jim Crow laws emanated from Massachusetts. We were not taught about the systematic persecution, and
in some instances, extinction of Native Americans by the Euro-
pean settlers. The library at Haut Gap, the all-black high school,
contained no books of the kind which one would have needed
to read to learn about the in depth race history of this country.

My matriculation through college and law school made me generally aware of racism in America. However, when I confronted the beast in the North for the first time in a legal setting, I was somewhat taken aback at its entrenchment. The viciousness exhibited in the manifestation of racism in the North, at least in this instance, was the same as what I had encountered in the South.

My dealings with Orange Memorial Hospital led me to ratify the truth of the noted author James Baldwin's reflection about blacks migrating to the North when he stated, *"They do not escape Jim Crow: they merely encounter another, not-less-deadly variety."* Race discrimination is not a southern problem, it is an American phenomenon. Perhaps Malcolm X said it best in a speech made in 1964 in Harlem when he declared, *"America is Mississippi. There's no such thing as a Mason-Dixon Line—its America. There's no such thing as the South—it's America."* Indeed, for my money, Mr. Shinn and the white administrative staff of Orange Memorial Hospital fortified my belief that the Mason-Dixon Line was a convenient, but extremely deceptive, geographic partition.

Discrimination by hospitals against black doctors was and is not unique to the South. In the early nineties, I represented a group of black doctors that had patient admitting privileges at Orange Memorial Hospital in Orange, New Jersey. This hospital was a for-profit enterprise. The Chief Executive Officer was a white man by the name of Shinn. The hospital serviced a population that was more than ninety percent people of color. Ninety-five percent of the hospital's administrative staff, excluding doctors, were Caucasians. Shinn presented himself as a no-nonsense administrator. He made decisions without the input from the forty percent professional medical staff whom were African-American or doctors of color.

My conversations with him gave me the distinct impression that he tried to govern the hospital with an iron fist.

All the doctors in the obstetrics and gynecology department were minorities. All of these doctors had admitting privileges at all the hospitals in the area. In the late eighties and early nineties, a patient that was admitted to a hospital by the treating physician, was a significant financial gain for the hospital. In regards to OB/GYN, a normal delivery would require that the mother be hospitalized for a minimum of two to three days. The hospital would bill for that patient's care at the rate of $2,000 to $3,000 a day. Additionally, the hospital reaped a fee of approximately $1,500 to $3,000 per day for the baby remaining in the hospital for those days before the mother was released. Thus, theoretically the hospital, Orange Memorial, could net $6,000 a day for 3 days for each delivery performed by the OB/GYN doctors at its facility. There were eight doctors in the OB/GYN department. They admitted to Orange Memorial approximately 150 to 200 patients each per year. That department accounted for approximately thirty-five percent plus of Orange Memorial's yearly profits. From about 1987 through the early nineties the chairmanship of the obstetrics and gynecological department rotated annually among the black gynecologists who were board-certified. That arrangement worked well among the physicians in that department. Practically, every one of the physicians that became chairman, could add a department chair to their resumes.

Shinn decided that there was a need for a permanent Chairman for gynecology and obstetrics. I sensed no dissension among the minority doctors about one of them becoming the permanent chairman. Shinn offered the position to none of those black doctors who had served as chairmen during the previous five years. All of them were qualified to be chairman. Shinn instead, decided that he wanted to offer the chairmanship to a Caucasian doctor from Missouri who had no experience as chairman of an obstetrics and gynecology department. As best I could determine, this white doctor's only experience in leadership was running an emergency clinic. When the black gynecologists and obstetricians got wind of Shinn's plan, they confronted him. Legitimately, the black doctors wanted to know why the chairmanship position was not advertised. If it had been properly advertised, one of these doctors would have applied for the position. Given the fact that all the board-certified OB/GYN physicians had rotated in the chairmanship position, it would appear that one of them would have been the logical choice. During the period of the black OB/GYN's rotating in and out of the chairmanship, Orange Memorial made money from the operation of that department. Because almost exclusively the black gynecologists referred their patients to Orange Memorial.

Shinn sternly asserted that it was his decision as to who would be the chairman of OB/GYN. He further told the group of black doctors that met with him, that if they did not like his choice, all of them were free to exercise the option to leave the hospital. Given the significant financial hit that Orange Memorial Hospital would take, how dumb was that position? There was an obvious disconnect between the ninety-five percent white administrative staff and the black doctors. More than ninety percent of patients of these OB/GYN were black. When Shinn refused to retreat from his stance of bringing in a Caucasian doctor, foreign to the community, two of those black OB/GYN doctors retained my services.

My first two encounters with Shinn went smoothly. I explained to him the concerns of my clients and that this was a matter that, with good faith efforts, should be resolved. On that point, I detected a certain chilliness in his responses. The words he chose to use in his telephonic conversations with me were raw and harsh and conveyed the notion of, *how dare these black sons of bitches challenge my authority.* My efforts to bring about an early resolution to this conflict fell on deaf ears. Shinn became even more obstinate. He virtually refused to resolve the matter. His resolution was, *I'm in control and I'll do what I damn well please.* We were at an impasse. He was determined to prove that he was the CEO and in charge. Legally, there was a very tenuous basis, if any, for bringing any kind of lawsuit against Shinn or the hospital to make him change his mind. After all, he was the CEO and hiring decisions were almost exclusively within his purview. After a couple weeks of more negotiations, it became strikingly clear that he was not willing to compromise in any respect.

The only thing that was going to bring Shinn to the bargaining table was public pressure and a dent in the bottom line, the finances. I told my clients to picket the hospital. And, oh did they do a good job. They made signs and started picketing the hospital for an hour a day during lunch time. That number grew from two to more than fifteen doctors within thirty days. Every day for a period of three months, the picket signs were in front of the hospital protesting about Shinn's decision not to advertise the job and wanting to give the chairmanship of the OB/GYN department to a Caucasian doctor with no experience. The local news media became my clients' allies. Community leaders, especially ministers and their congregations, joined in the protest. Some became all too happy to carry a picket sign with these doctors. The number of protesters, peacefully exercising their First Amendment rights, remained solid, a minimum of fifty to seventy-five persons per day. It was a splendid site of black people telling the all-white administrative staff of Orange Memorial Hospital, "You cannot disrespect our black doctors." This was truly a flashback to the Civil Rights marches of the 1960s and seventies. Still obstinate, Shinn brought the white doctor from Missouri to meet with my clients. During that meeting, the doctor from Missouri agreed with my clients. He said he should not become the chair of the OB/GYN department. Among other things, he was not familiar with the culture of the community that Orange Memorial served.

As the protest grew in size, there were calls for Shinn's resignation. Other black OB/GYN doctors began to decrease the number of patients they admitted to Orange Memorial. As a result, the hospital began to lose a significant amount of money. Shinn and the members of the white administrative staff had completely miscalculated the reaction of the black doctors and the community to his stance. The community, doctors, patients, and church leaders viewed Shinn's attitude as racially motivated. The constant press inquiries and coverage painted a picture of Shinn as being a racist white man who did not understand the community which the hospital served.

There were a few white doctors on staff at the hospital. Many of them supported my clients in private. Very few, if any of them, would reinforce, publicly, their private views. Soon enough, at a general staff meeting for all physicians, there was almost a universal call for this matter to end. The press had laid bare the insensitivity and callousness of the white administrative staff's practices against the black patients and these doctors. Shinn, by this time, had lost whatever credibility he had with the community and black doctors. Because of his unremitting stance, the Board of Directors for the hospital terminated him. But the Board let this matter linger for too long. People in the community lost trust in Orange Memorial.

Efforts to reconstitute the hospital failed miserably. Within four years from the date of the first protest, Orange Memorial Hospital closed its door. I never quite understood why the administration and Board of Directors of Orange Memorial did not see the need to accommodate the black doctors and the very people that it served. The lesson for me from this case was that unity among protesters will bring about the desired results. The togetherness of the doctors and the community demonstrated to the Board of Directors, and all who would listen, that they were a force to be reckoned with. The Board of Directors chose to continue to back the asinine policy of Orange Memorial's administrative staff in condoning racism as opposed to being financially viable. After the marginal profits that Orange Memorial was making shrunk and dissipated, the board's action was like closing the barn door after the horse had left a stable.

CHAPTER 7

The Reverend Jennings

One of the most reprehensible attributes that can be attached to the Prosecutor's Office is how the office uses its enhanced power to punish black and poor people for exercising their constitutional rights. In a perfect world, the Prosecutor's Office exists for the purpose of seeking justice. A democratic society works best when those who are charged with enforcing the law carry out that mandate without regard to race, color, or creed. It is particularly heinous when they use their power to prosecute a citizen because of their race in our judicial system. Here, in South Carolina, the Prosecutor's Office is divided into circuits. That means that more than one county can make up a circuit. In the Ninth Judicial Circuit, which I am familiar with, the powers of that office have been used for the purpose of silencing black people, especially those who have challenged the improper application of the law in regards to them.

One local civil rights leader was considered a thorn in the side of the political establishment. He was a well-known minister that had a very loyal and all-black congregation. In an attempt to get equal treatment for his parishioners and other African-Americans, he along with some of the older retired members, would, on many occasions, picket banks, grocery stores, and other white-owned businesses in response their racist treatment of black people. There was a concerted effort from the Prosecutor's Office to grab hold of any mistake, that they thought amounted to a violation of law so that they could prosecute or embarrass Rev. Marcus Jennings or his family. Fortunately, for him, no such opportunity arose because he was as straight as an arrow. The Prosecutor's Office couldn't, with the hands of injustice, damage or persecute Rev. Jennings. To say that this office was extremely bothered by Rev. Jennings' local Civil Rights activity, would be an understatement. They had a section, I was told, in their office that would scrutinize any police report that reflected the last name of Jennings as the defendant. They were determined to either prosecute Rev. Jennings or someone related to him. That's how mad they were at the good Reverend.

The Reverend had a son, Marcus Jennings Jr., who was not as religiously grounded as his father. The Prosecutor's Office made an attempt to embarrass Rev. Jennings through the prosecution of his son, Marcus. Marcus had a pension for drinking. It has to be noted that the law enforcement officials played an instrumental part in the scheme. Normally, the police authority, through one of its officers, would arrest the family member or relative of the person they seek to silence. That arrest would result in a felonious charge. A felony is a crime committed that is punishable by more than a year in jail. In this instance, Rev. Jennings never gave the police any reason to arrest him. However, I am persuaded that police knew the names of all of Jennings' relatives and immediate family.

Rev. Marcus Jennings never sought the limelight. He was a minister who saw the plight of an oppressed people, and to due to his calling, wanted to do something to alleviate that condition. Those who were in opposition, namely the white power structure, saw him as a threat to the dominance that they exhibited on a daily basis when it came to the lives of black people. They could never find anything to remotely connect him to a criminal enterprise, violation of city ordinances, or state law. But Lord knows they did try. Having no success with arresting and embarrassing Rev. Jennings, they turned to his family members.

On the corner of Broad and King Streets in the City of Charleston, South Carolina, a beer distributor truck was stopped. Rev. Jennings' son, Marcus, slightly tapped, with his car, the rear bumper of the beer truck. The City of Charleston Police Department was called to investigate this alleged accident. There is no doubt that Marcus Jennings, Jr. was tipsy. The city police officer arrived at the supposed accident scene an hour and a half (ninety minutes) later, presumably because there was no injury or damage to either vehicle or the occupants. About ten minutes before the police officer arrived, Marcus Jennings, Jr. left the scene and was on his way home. The beer truck driver wrote down the license plate number for the car that Marcus was driving. That number was given to the police officer who immediately ran it through the State Department of Motor Vehicles only to find that the car was registered to Marcus Jennings, Jr. An all-points bulletin was issued for the car and its driver.

Within minutes, Marcus Jennings, Jr.'s car was spotted and stopped by a city prosecutor. That city prosecutor had put a blue light on the top of his car to stop Marcus' car. The city prosecutor never got out of his car. A few minutes later, uniform police officers arrived. They arrested Marcus Jennings, Jr., charging him with leaving the scene of an accident, DUI, as well as assaulting an officer while resisting arrest. Resisting arrest is a felony that carries prison time of up to ten years.

Immediately, after Rev. Jennings engaged my services to represent Marcus Jennings, Jr., I was determined that this scheme by the City of Charleston Police Department and the Prosecutor's Office to embarrass Rev. Marcus Jennings, Sr., would be exposed and unravel. The laws of South Carolina, at that time, required that before a collision between two vehicles can be deemed an accident, there must be physical damage to at least one of the vehicles. There was no damage to Marcus Jennings, Jr.'s car or the beer truck. Logically, then there could be no accident that occurred. If no accident had occurred, my client could not have been charged with leaving the scene of an accident nor would there be probable cause for his arrest. The beer company provided me with the letter indicating that there was no damage done to its truck. I believe, to this day, that the Prosecutor's Office was going to do everything in its power to put Marcus Jennings, Jr. in jail for the maximum ten years. I presented my theory of the case to one of the top prosecutors in that office who was assigned to handle this case. My arguments regarding the law and the facts of this case fell on deaf ears. It was as if they were determined, no matter what the law was, to do harm to Marcus Jennings, Jr. and thereby punish his father, Marcus Jennings, Sr. If at all possible, I was not going to allow that to happen.

During that time, the solicitor or (prosecutor) had the very broad discretion in determining which judge would try the case. Marcus Jennings, Jr.'s case was appointed to a judge from upstate South Carolina who was assigned to try criminal cases in Charleston County that week. This judge was still fighting the Civil War and did not know, based on his prior reputation, that the South had lost. When it came to black defendants, he was mean, intemperate, and displayed characteristics that demonstrated his unfitness to wear the robe of justice. The solicitor's office scheduled this case to be started on Wednesday of that week. The case before our case ended about mid-day on Wednesday. The jury in that case went to lunch prior to beginning its deliberations. On the way back from lunch, one of the police officers that testified in that case told a juror that the City of Charleston Police Department worked hard on that case and they need to find the defendant guilty. This comment was relayed to the judge who was going to try the Jennings case next. Unfortunately for the Solicitor, but fortunately for Mr. Jennings, all hell broke loose. That judge had the police officer arrested and the solicitor's office, as well as the City of Charleston Police Department, went into a tizzy. Mr. Jennings' case was not going to be tried that day.

The next day, Mr. Jennings' case was called for trial, but before a different judge. As I practiced law, it became routine for me to file constitutional motions to have cases dismissed and/or evidence suppressed because of the inappropriate conduct on the part of law enforcement officials that violated the defendant's constitutional rights. A motion of that caliber, one to suppress, was filed in Mr. Jennings' case. Those motions filed in a criminal case are heard by the judge outside of the presence of the jury before the trial begins. Oddly enough, as I entered into the courtroom with Marcus Jennings, Sr., as well as a number of his parishioners and other interested community officials, the initial solicitor who was assigned to handle this case for the state was not present. Being in combat mode, I did not give much attention to that fact because I was determined that nothing was going to throw me off of my game plan in terms of defending Marcus Jennings, Jr. The presiding judge asked if there were any pretrial motions to be heard. I answered, "Yes there are, Your Honor." In rifling through his file, he stated, "I will hear the Motion to Dismiss first." The courtroom was packed with black and white people. The clerk of court, who was rarely present at a criminal trial, was also there. There were also a number of white lawyers present.

When asked to proceed by the presiding judge, I argued that this stop was a violation of the constitutional right of the Defendant Marcus Jennings, Jr. I continued, *"Under the laws of South Carolina before one can be charged with leaving the scene of an accident, the statue requires that physical damage be done to one or both of the vehicles involved in the accident."* I presented to the court a sworn statement from the company that owned the beer truck, which clearly stated that there was no physical damage done to the beer truck. A picture was passed up to the judge, which clearly illustrated that there was no damage done to Mr. Jennings' car. Therefore, there was no accident. If there was no accident, which this evidence establishes, there can be no charge of leaving the scene of an accident. The police authorities, especially the city prosecutor, had no reason to stop his vehicle. Thus, my client's arrest was unconstitutional and unlawful.

The judge then asked the solicitor to present their argument. Much to my pleasant surprise, a young female Caucasian attorney got up from the solicitor's table to present the argument. That let me know that the prosecutor's office had no faith in this case. They knew that this was not going to fly, in terms of Mr. Jennings being convicted, because the thought process was if the case was lost, that loss would not be chalked up to the top prosecutor in their office. The young lawyer got up and started arguing about the meaning of the word damage. Her argument was that it was an ambiguous term and could be construed to mean a number of different things. So offended was I by this nonsensical argument, I jumped to my feet for the purpose of informing the court that criminal Law 101 teaches any lawyer that criminal statutes are to be strictly construed. However, before I could utter those words, the judge said, *"Sit down Mr. Brown. I'll handle this part."* This judge asked the young female lawyer if she were serious about that argument. Before she could answer, the duly elected Solicitor of Charleston County, stood up and said, *"We are going to put on the stand the City of Charleston prosecutor who stopped Mr. Jennings to prove that he was driving under the influence of alcohol."* The Trial judge then said to the prosecutor, *"I can't tell you how to present your case but, if the city prosecutor, who is not authorized by statute to have a blue light testifies that he put that blue light on the top of his car to stop Mr. Jennings, he is going to be arrested for violation of the South Carolina criminal statute which says that only duly licensed police officers can have blue lights on their car."*

This chief prosecutor for Charleston County conferred with the other prosecutors at his table and came over to me and whispered in my ears, *"Ed, we are going to drop back and punt on this one."* In my mind I screamed out, *"Unball your fist motherf--er, you didn't want this fight from the beginning."* The case was dismissed by the judge. There was a quiet jubilation in the courtroom. As I was packing up my materials from the defense table, a Caucasian lawyer approached me and said, *"You have just embarrassed the Solicitor's Office and rightfully so."* That comment was totally unexpected, but true. Even the clerk of court came to me in the hallway and said, *"Congratulations, the right thing happened in the courtroom today."* From that day forward, I developed a tremendous degree of respect for that presiding judge because, in this instance, he was fair and was not a part of the system that was designed to stifle people who were criminally punished because they protested the oppression. Marcus Jennings, Jr. did not come to my office again for representation in any criminal matter.

CHAPTER 8

Josh Johnson–Enlisted in U.S. Navy and Arrested for Robbery

There were occasions in my practice that required the use of every strategy that could be legally employed to prevent the prosecution of an innocent defendant. I was retained to represent a young brilliant black guy, named Josh Johnson, who was an enlisted member of the United States Navy. He was a crewman on a ship that was stationed in Charleston, South Carolina at the Naval Base. Near the naval base, there had been a series of armed robberies. The local law enforcement agency got a description of the robber. Although that description was in no way definitive, they were determined to make an arrest. The predominant feature of the robber, as the police officers said in their reports, was that the suspect was a black male about 5'10" tall. This occurred in the late eighties and there were no surveillance cameras or any other video devices available to give a better account of how the suspect looked other than being black. Mr. Johnson did not remotely match the description of the person who had committed these robberies.

One night he left the ship for the purpose of meeting some of his civilian friends at a bar near the Naval Base. That bar was located near the area where the robberies had been committed. While patrolling the area, a police officer approached my client asking for identification. He was not wearing his naval uniform, although that would not have mattered to these Gestapo-like officers. He was walking and refused the officer's request to present identification. The officer immediately detained Mr. Johnson and called for backup. Mr. Johnson was handcuffed and placed in the back of the police officer's cruiser. When the backup arrived, they questioned Mr. Johnson about the robberies that had occurred. Josh insisted that he knew nothing about any robberies and was on his way to a club to meet his friends. They told him that he fit the description of the person who had committed the robberies. Mr. Johnson was black, but 6'4" tall.

That detail did not seem to, in any manner, interfere with the design of these police officers on that night. They were determined to arrest someone for these robberies. Unfortunately, on this evening that person was Mr. Johnson. They took him to the police station for the purpose of interrogation. They read him his Miranda Rights and he signed a statement indicating that those rights had been read to him. During that time, the 1980s, law enforcement authorities did not have to tape or do an audio of the interrogation efforts. According to Josh, he was kept in the interrogation room for more than six hours. He never admitted that he participated in any robberies. There, obviously, was a serious push coming from the executive level of the local law enforcement to arrest someone for these robberies. Mr. Johnson was arrested and charged with armed robbery.

It was common practice then for officers to lie in police reports stating that suspects admitted that they had committed crimes being investigated. These police officers, in their report, insisted that Mr. Johnson confessed to one of the robberies. Josh came from a good family and never had any previous encounters with law enforcement. He was well thought of by his fellow crew members and the command structure on the ship, especially the Executive Officer. After being hired by the family to represent Josh, I began to do my investigation regarding these charges. It was not lost on me that if he was convicted, he would face a substantial amount of time in jail. Also, his military career would end. After Mr. Johnson was arrested, the robberies stopped. That gave the prosecutors footing to believe that those robberies were committed by my client. My investigation led me to talk to a number of his shipmates, as well as the executive officer of the ship to which Josh was assigned. That executive officer thought that Josh was the prototypical Navy person and was not convinced that Josh Johnson was the person who had committed these robberies. During one of my interviews with the executive officer of the ship, it was revealed to me that he was a college roommate of the prosecutor.

About a year after his arrest, the case was going to be called for trial by the prosecutor. After being provided with a day certain for the trial, I sent out subpoenas for witnesses that I believed would attest to the sterling reputation of Mr. Johnson. My thought was that a jury would not convict him solely on the words of two police officers that said that he confessed to them about these robberies if there were witnesses who would attest to his character and that the act of committing a robbery would be unlike my client. One of the persons I subpoenaed for trial was the Executive Officer of the Naval Vessel, who spoke so highly of Josh.

I then learned that the ship to which Josh was assigned, was going out to sea for trials the day before the trial and would not return for a month. I had my process server to serve the subpoena on the Executive Officer, as well as the other witnesses that were not members of the military. About four hours after the subpoena was served, I got a call from the Executive Officer. He told me that the ship was due to leave port the following day and he would not be at trial notwithstanding the fact that he been subpoenaed. I informed him that perhaps a subpoena could not stop the departure of the United States destroyer leaving ports for sea trials, but he still had to honor the subpoena.

On the day of trial, the trial judge, as this judge usually did, brought all the lawyers in his chambers to determine whether or not there would be any issues in going forward with the trial. The trial judge was John Elrod. Elrod was about 6'5" and every bit of 280 pounds. He had gray hair and wore black rim eye glasses. Because of the sheer baritone nature of his voice, this judge did not need a microphone while in the courtroom. His presence, more so than usual, dominated the room. I had appeared before him on previous occasions in what are called motion hearings. To me he was very thoughtful and knew the law. I didn't detect in him the racial animus that was sometimes painfully evident in other white judges. The most impressive character trait about Judge Elrod was his no-nonsense approach in most courtroom proceedings. He expected the lawyers to be adequately prepared in the presentation of their cases on behalf of the clients. Anything less than that would incur his wrath. I never experienced that because I always tried to be prepared. Some lawyers referred to him as a *"cowboy,"* because he pretty much did anything he wanted to do from the bench and very few lawyers had the balls to challenge him. I believe that he would have conducted the trial in a fair manner. However, if my client was found guilty, he would have given him the maximum sentence.

I informed the judge that, on behalf of the defendant, I issued a subpoena to the executive officer of the ship to which Josh was assigned and the executive officer would not be coming to trial. The judge became enraged. He stated to one of the assistant prosecutors assigned to try the case for the state, in clear and certain terms, that when the executive officer got back in the Port, a warrant for his arrest would be served and he was going to *"lock his ass up."* The judge further said *"Charlie Simons,"* a federal judge, *"might let his ass out, but I am going to put his behind in jail for ignoring a subpoena that was duly issued for his presence in this criminal trial."* One of the assistant prosecutors hurriedly left the judge's chamber. The judge told the bailiff to go outside the courtroom, after the trial would have started, and call the name of the Executive Officer three times. As we were about to get up from our seats to leave his chambers to start the trial, the prosecutor came in and said to the judge, *"Your Honor, you will not need to start this trial because we are going to dismiss this case."* It became clear to me that the prosecutor did not want his former roommate put in jail by Judge Elrod. We went into open court and the case was dismissed on the record.

CHAPTER 9

The Racing Case

Orangeburg County is a very rural area located in the middle of South Carolina. There is nothing particularly unique about Orangeburg, other than the fact that two of the state's historically black institutions of higher learning are located within its boundaries. It is not well populated and most of its inhabitants are black and poor whites. There are a number of past times which the residents engage in as entertainment. One such endeavor is car racing. Young men, and in some cases women, would race their cars on the rural back roads for the purpose of bragging rights about who had the fastest car. This was in 1982, and I was a young lawyer when I was hired to represent a defendant in a racing case in Orangeburg County. Racing, on roads in any county, is illegal and a felony. Racing is also very ingrained in Southern culture and practiced by all groups. It is not an enterprise restricted to any ethnicity. I am not a racing fan and I have never quite understood what joy anyone would receive from driving a car at an extravagantly high rate of speed on a two-lane highway competing against another vehicle. To my mind this can be, and in some instances was, a literal fatality waiting to happen.

Nonetheless, the tradition, albeit illegal, continues to exist for sure in the South. The young man, Charles Hansen, was accused of committing the felony of racing on Rural Highway 4 in Orangeburg County. I am not sure that the police officer who arrested Mr. Hansen actually caught my client in the act of racing his vehicle on that highway. The police report included no license plate number of the vehicle that was racing on the day in question. As I remember, the police report stated that there was a yellow GTO with chrome bumpers participating in this criminal activity. It is true that Mr. Hansen owned a yellow GTO with chrome bumpers. However, neither the police officer or any of the witnesses he claimed he talked to could place Mr. Hansen himself at the scene of the race. Mr. Hansen and his father both told me during my initial interview with them that he was not at the scene of the race. He further told me that he knew the race was going to occur, but someone else drove his car during the race. That person was his first cousin, Charles Joyner.

The trial judge, John Aiken, was an absolute terror in the courtroom. During that time the Circuit Solicitor had the right to call criminal cases for trial in the order that he deemed appropriate. However, John Aiken would come to that county and usurp (from the Solicitor) the trial docket for criminal cases. He would then call the cases that he wanted to go to trial. The common joke was that when John came to Orangeburg County as the trial judge to try criminal cases, the duly elected Solicitor, Steven Harte, would become ill and not show up for court that week or term of court. While I feared him, I was not afraid of him. If he disliked you, he would make your life hell during a trial. He was truly from a different era. His judicial temperament was dubious at best. He had a reputation of getting up during a trial and smoking a cigarette in the doorway that led to the courtroom from the judge's chambers while the trial was ongoing. I had heard stories from lawyers that he was not in the courtroom for brief moments during trial. As was routine with most judges before trial, the prosecutor and the defense attorney would be invited into the judge's chambers for the purpose of addressing any issues that might come up during the course of the trial. In some instances, there would be negotiations about a possible plea deal and any sentences that might be imposed by the judge.

Prior to Mr. Hansen's case being called for trial, the prosecutor and I met with Judge Aiken. He then proceeded to tell me that my client should plead guilty. It was a simple racing case and he was not going to give him any time in jail. I responded that my client was not guilty and it would be ethically wrong for me to tell him to plead guilty. This case was called for trial on a Thursday morning. I later came to understand that this was the last case on the criminal trial docket for that week. A guilty plea would mean that Judge Aiken could leave early that day and not work on Friday. He continued to press me to make my client plead guilty. A guilty plea to a felony, would amount to the client being saddled with a criminal record for the rest of his life. That would jeopardize him getting a job that required a background check. This effort went on for about thirty minutes and I continued to resist. I finally told him that I cannot make someone plead guilty who is not guilty and if he was guilty, he would not need my services. He could, by himself, come to the court to plead guilty and ask for mercy when being sentenced. Aiken's teeth began to grit and his face became red. I will admit that I was nervous, because if a jury found my client guilty, Judge Aiken was going to sentence him to two years in prison.

The one thing I definitely had in my favor was that the defendant was black, I was black, and the jury panel was majority black.

Orangeburg was one of the few counties in the State of South Carolina that had a substantial black population. When we selected the jury, I was lucky enough to get four black people seated on the jury. During the selection of the jury, each side, the defendant and the solicitor, is given a total of six strikes. The prosecutor used all six of his strikes to remove black jurors from the jury panel. Until 1986—when the United States Supreme Court ruled in a case called *Batson v. Kentucky,* that in a criminal case, jurors could not be removed by the prosecutor because of their race—that kind of conduct on the part of the prosecutor, was routine. My thought was that I could either get a hung jury or an acquittal. But I knew it was not going to be easy, because I would incur the wrath of Judge Aiken at some point during the trial.

From opening to closing arguments, the case took approximately eight hours to complete. The prosecutor made his closing argument to the jury first. He didn't have a very good case, to the extent that they had no witnesses that could place my client in the yellow GTO on the date that the racing occurred. He argued before the jury for conviction for a total of approximately fifteen minutes. When it became my turn to speak to the jury, the judge informed me that I only had twenty minutes to conduct closing arguments and for every minute I went over twenty, I would be held in contempt of court, fined $100 per minute, and possibly be jailed. It now became clear to me what his fury was going to be. I decided in my mind that I was going to argue until I felt comfortable that the jury understood the defendant's defense in this case. It took me forty-five minutes to present, in closing argument, our assessment of the state's case and to urge the jury that they should return a verdict of not guilty. I knew then that if I had to be held in contempt, then I would have had an opportunity to have my day in court for this court-imposed rule of limiting my arguments to the jury in a criminal case.

Also, I was aware of the rules of ethics that governs lawyers' conduct, which states a lawyer is supposed to represent his client zealously. After my argument to the jury, Judge Aiken charged the jury as to what the law was and how to apply them to the facts of this case. He was not happy with me arguing more than the twenty minute limit he had imposed. After the jury retired to the jury room to commence their deliberations, I was expecting, at the very least, a harsh admonition, if not being held in contempt, and perhaps jailed. He then, as the trial judge is supposed to do, asked if there were any additional matters from the prosecutor or from the defense attorney. We both responded that there were none. He then hit the gavel and said, *"the court will be in recess."* At that point, I thought in my mind, *this son-of-a bitch is going to impose whatever penalty he can on me and my client if the jury comes back with a guilty verdict.* The jury stayed out a total of one hour and thirty-six minutes. It returned a verdict of not guilty. The judge dismissed the jury, and on the way out, I thanked them for rendering justice to my client on that day. Nothing more was said by the judge regarding this possible contempt of court for arguing more than twenty minutes before the jury. On that day, I learned that you can't go along to get along if you are to do what is right.

CHAPTER 10

Cummings Case

This day began as any other day. However, at about 10 a.m., I received a telephone call from a young woman whose husband had been killed by a police officer. I secured from her, as much facts as I could over the telephone before giving her an appointment to come to my office and have a face-to-face interview. This was one of the most vile set of facts that I had ever encountered, up to this point in my legal career.

My client's husband, while driving his car, was stopped by a county police officer, purportedly, because there was a warrant for his arrest. After the stop, the police officer detained the client's husband for a period in excess of forty-five minutes, waiting on confirmation from the Sheriff's Office that there was a valid warrant for the arrest of this young black man. Of course, the police officer was white and had been employed at the Sheriff's Office as a Deputy less than two years. During the stop, my client's husband remained seated in his car. The police officer, after exiting his car to inform my client's husband why he was stopping him, went back to his car and stayed there, waiting for confirmation of an arrest warrant for Mr. Cummings. The twenty-two-year-old black man decided that he would drive off because he wanted to be on time for work. The white police officer proceeded to exit his car and shot into Mr. Cummings' car four times as he drove away, causing Mr. Cummings' car to overturn and run into a fence at the end of the street. All four of the bullets struck Mr. Cummings. He died instantaneously.

It was later revealed, after we filed a civil lawsuit, that there was no warrant for Mr. Cummings' arrest. In fact, during the forty-five minutes when Mr. Cummings was being detained by the white police officer, a white female Magistrate Court judge was signing a document which indicated that Mr. Cummings failed to appear at court for a traffic ticket. The problem with this story, as I later found out, was that there was no traffic ticket issued to Mr. Cummings. It is impossible to be charged with failure to appear before the court for a traffic ticket if none was issued.

To this day, the factual contours of this case are still embedded in my soul. Mr. Cummings was murdered at the hands of a white Deputy Sheriff in cahoots with a white female Magistrate for no other reason than being black. At the time of his death, he had been married for less than a year. Yet, again, another black life snuffed out at the whim of a white Deputy Sheriff and a crooked white female Magistrate.

I felt it incumbent upon me to do something to try to bring some form of justice or raise the community level of consciousness as to the unfairness of the tragic death that befell this young black man. I knew that the judicial system would not levy any criminal sanctions against either the Magistrate or the Deputy Sheriff.

Although the case was settled for a sufficient amount of money, there was still a void in my soul that compelled me to try to do more, try to do something else that would bring some form of accountability for this tragic and unnecessary death. Every time I had a face-to-face conference with my client, I could see in her eyes a certain emptiness as a result of the murder of her husband. The state law virtually insulated this officer from prosecution for the death of this black man. Up to that point, the late 1980s, no prosecutor in the state had ever tried to indict a white police officer for killing a black man.

If I could get a finding from a state or county official that the cause of my client's husband's death was an unlawful killing, then maybe the United States Department of Justice could be requested to do an investigation to determine whether my client's husband's civil rights were violated. That was a long-shot at best. The only county official that could make such an unlawful killing ruling was the county coroner's office. Armed with that thought, I requested a coroner's inquest into the death of my client's husband.

Coroners are popularly elected officials. There is no formal educational requirement necessary for one to run for the coroner's office. In the eighties, they were usually persons without any college education.

On the date of the inquest, I felt a calmness as I travelled the eighty-four miles by car to the courthouse in that County. I was oblivious to any concerns for my personal safety. While I knew what I wanted to accomplish in the inquest, my tunnel mindset to attain some form of justice for my client left unaddressed any other concerns. This county had a Chief Law Enforcement official, I was later told, who tolerated or perhaps even encouraged the circulation of the N-word, jungle bunny jokes, and other racially-demeaning insults of blacks on its official office letterhead. No disciplinary actions were imposed upon the white officers responsible for creating and circulating those despicable flyers or handouts. Even if those revelations were made known to me before the inquest, that would not have stopped me from demanding or being present at the inquest. During that time, fear was not a companion of mine.

As my client and I came to the courtroom where the inquest was going to be held, there was a visible presence of white citizens and law enforcement officers. These many officers were fully dressed in their uniforms with weapons in their holsters. While I knew the policy in regards to police officers having their weapons at a coroner's inquest, I thought it odd that all twenty-five to thirty of them would have weapons in the courtroom. There were no criminals to be guarded in the upcoming proceeding. No threats had been issued against any law enforcement officials. Perhaps, I thought, this was their way of intimidating me and my client from moving forward with the matter at hand. At this sight, my client became a bit unnerved. My words to her were, *"We are going to have this inquest and nothing or no one will deny us this day from going forth."* There were no more than fifteen black people in the courtroom. On my way up to the courtroom, I saw two black law enforcement officials.

The hearing started at 6 p.m. I didn't expect much in the way of the finding of an unlawful killing from this coroner's judge. As she, the judge, started the proceedings, I noticed her disdainful look at me and my client. Her demeanor was so obvious in that it conveyed the notion of *how dare you and your client trouble me with making a determination as to whether or not this was an unlawful killing.* None of the witnesses called to testify verified the law enforcement version of what occurred prior to this white officer drawing his weapon and shooting my client's husband four times as he drove away. There was no credible evidence that, as the officer claimed, my client's husband, with his car, dragged him before he discharged four shots from his weapon fatally injuring the driver.

Even if that testimony was believable, my client's husband was driving away from the officer as he discharged his weapon. There was no need to kill this black man on that day. *The one witness that testified about Mr. Cummings' failure to appear for the traffic ticket, could not recall any previous arrest warrant being issued for Mr. Cummings (or anyone else for that matter) because the witness did not appear in traffic court.* I tried my best during cross-examination to exact a pound of flesh from every witness the other side presented for the purpose of justifying this killing. This was not an evening to take prisoners. The hearing went on for three and a half hours. As I expected, the coroner took the matter under advisement. She did not render a decision that evening.

After the hearing, my client and some of her family members conversed with me for about ten to fifteen minutes while we were still in the courthouse. As I exited the courthouse, I was approached by a black deputy sheriff. I didn't know him but he knew me. He said, *"Mr. Brown, when you get in your car, I will follow you in my vehicle. We are going to give you an escort to the county lines. Don't be nervous."* I felt reasonably assured that this officer who looked like me was going to get me to the Sumter County lines. But my mind began to race as to what would happen after that. If I got to Interstate 95, I would be okay. In the meantime, I had a flashback to the time my black classmates and I were cornered in the bathroom at St. John's High School by the white gang. I had a weapon, a snug nose 38 revolver in my car's glove compartment. That might not be enough to stop those who would try to do harm to me, but it would inflict damage on any prospective attacker. After I got to Interstate 95, I drove the speed limit all the way home. I was not going to give any law enforcement official a reason to stop my vehicle.

The coroner's report was filed. Much to my disappointment, although not unexpected, there was no finding of an unlawful killing. I consoled myself. I knew I did my best in trying to bring about some form of punishment to the police officer who unlawfully took the life of this young black man.

CHAPTER 11

Being Prepared

The success rate for prosecutors is approximately eighty-five percent in criminal cases that are tried before a jury. My strategy was always to file as many constitutional motions that could be reasonably argued to a judge to get the case dismissed before it got to the jury. That required an extensive amount of preparation through reading case law on the constitutional violation that I was trying to argue to the court that required the case to be dismissed. Not only that, my argument had to be precise and persuasive. On numerous occasions I prevailed at those motion hearings because I was more prepared to persuade the court of the merits of my constitutional arguments than the prosecutor. And when I was not successful in convincing the trial court of the dismissal of the case because of a constitutional violation, I would have created, in part, a well-reasoned factual and law record for the appellate courts if that became necessary.

In one such instance, I was hired by the lead attorney to argue the constitutional Motion to Suppress Evidence seized by the police as a result of an unlawful arrest. The client came to Charleston by train. Law enforcement, as they claim, had a tip that my client was transporting a large amount of marijuana from up north to this area. They didn't have a good description of the person, who later turned out to be my client, who was transporting the drugs. A black man got off of the train carrying a duffle bag. The law enforcement officials stopped and detained him for almost two and one-half hours. They didn't have a warrant to search any of his luggage. While they told him that he was not under arrest, they also refused to allow him to leave. They did, after almost three hours, get a warrant from a judge to search his luggage and the search revealed a large quantity of marijuana in one of his bags.

At the suppression hearing before the Circuit Court judge, I argued, vociferously, that his constitutional rights were violated. The crux of my argument was that the police authorities could not detain him for almost three hours while they scurried about to get a search warrant for his luggage. I further argued that refusing to allow him to leave, was in fact an arrest. The Constitution does not allow one to be detained for three hours by law enforcement officials and having those same officials, through the prosecutor, argue that the defendant was not under arrest and therefore it was okay to detain him while they obtained a search warrant. The Circuit Court judge ruled against us on the trial court level, but a good factual record was created for the Supreme Court to review. The case was appealed to the South Carolina Supreme Court and that court reversed the ruling of the Circuit Court judge when it held that the evidence seized, because of this illegal arrest, should have been suppressed.

Some who read what was recited above will summarily conclude that a drug dealer got to go free. But I can, at that notion with fundamental truth, remind all that the U. S. Constitution is there to be observed and reckoned with. No one, not even law enforcement officials, can violate the rights secured to each citizen by the Constitution in order to obtain a conviction. That is what I believe was preserved that day and it should be of no moment that the defendant went free. What is more important is that the mandates of the United States Constitution (against illegal search and seizure) were observed. The arguments and the law of that case as stated by the Supreme Court is taught to police trainees at the Criminal Justice Academy in Columbia, South Carolina.

CHAPTER 12

High School Athlete

As is the practice in most of America and particularly in the South, African-Americans are stopped by law enforcement with impunity. A couple of the favorite tricks used for stopping persons of color while driving, is that *"the vehicle taillight is not operating properly," "the driver improperly changed lanes," "the license plate light is out,"* among many other made up reasons that are obviously fabricated and racially motivated. In one instance, a police officer that I was questioning at a preliminary hearing actually had the nerve and gall to admit that the reason he had stopped my client, a black male, was because he was driving a late-model 735 BMW vehicle.

While there are many criminal cases in which I represented black defendants, there was one, among many, that I found to be incredibly troubling. One such case was a young African-American man who was a high school senior and stellar athlete. He also had the academic acuity that matched, if not, superseded with athletic skills. His talents made him destined to be accepted by a number of Division I college football or basketball programs.

His notoriety invited scrutiny from the town and county law enforcement officials. His complexion was what I would call teacake mahogany brown. His physique was chiseled. He was necessarily, as is often the case in high school, the object of many female suitors. A number of them were white. On a Friday night, after football season, he was on his way to a fast-food joint with two white girls in his car. The Summerville Police officer turned on his blue lights. My client, with the two white girls in the car, pulled the car over to a well-lit area for the purpose of determining why he was being stopped by the police officer. This officer, a white male, immediately asked my client for his driver's license and registration. No reason was given to my client as to why he was being stopped. The police officer then proceeded to tell my client that there was an odor of marijuana coming from his vehicle. That was stunning to my client to the extent that he had never smoked marijuana. This white police officer then demanded that my client step out of the vehicle. No such demand was made of the two white females who were passengers in my client's vehicle. After patting down this young man for contrabands and/or a weapon, which the officer could legally do, he told my client to stand at the rear of his car and the front of the officer's patrol vehicle. My client dutifully obeyed. The officer then opened the driver's side door of the vehicle my client was operating and claimed he found a couple of marijuana joints below the driver's seat. In black parlance, this is called driving while black and having evidence planted in your vehicle.

It was of no concern to this white police officer that he had no actual probable cause to stop and search the car that this young black man was operating. In this case, in the eyes of this police officer, this young black guy was guilty of being black, athletic, and academically gifted as well as consorting with white females. He was charged with possession of marijuana. If found guilty, his chances for an athletic and an academic scholarship would have been severely hampered.

In cases of this caliber, one of the first things that I always did in representing my clients was to request discovery. In a case call *Brady v. Maryland,* the United States Supreme Court said that it is mandatory that prosecutorial authority and law enforcement provide all evidence to the defendant that constituted a factual basis for the stop and arrest of the defendant. Invariably, the second thing I did was to request a preliminary hearing. A preliminary hearing, theoretically, is held for the purpose of a low-level judge, usually not one with a college education, to determine whether there is enough evidence for the case to be bound over to the criminal courts for prosecution. On rare occasions, the preliminary hearing court judge would dismiss the charges. But under the laws of the state of South Carolina, the prosecutor still can move forward with the case in criminal court if he or she so chooses. The main strategic purpose for which I would use the preliminary hearings, is to try to obtain conflicting testimony from the testifying law enforcement official and the incident report. If the case proceeded to trial, nothing is better for a defendant than to get law enforcement to give different versions of the facts, from their side of the fence. Juries are more often than not persuaded to view the testifying police officers' versions of what occurred with severe skepticism especially if there is a significant conflict between the two versions. In those days, the early 2000s, police officers did not wear body cameras.

In this case, the two white females were not charged with any crime. They were allowed to call their parents to come pick them up. My client was taken to jail, photographed, and fingerprinted. I was prepared to blow the roof off this case on behalf of my client. My thought process was yet again, you have a young black man that the judicial system was prepared to persecute.

While the criminal matter was still pending, about six months later, his mother called and informed me that her son, my client, had been in a rather severe automobile accident. The mother told me the car that struck her son's vehicle crossed the median of a two-lane highway colliding with her son's car almost head on. The driver of the other car was charged with DUI. This was a clear case of liability from which her son could have reaped a substantial monetary settlement. I wondered, not aloud to her, why I was not contacted about representation of her son in that case. When the conversation finally got to that point, I simply asked the mother why she didn't contact me to represent him. The mother informed me that they had contracted with a white lawyer because she didn't believe I could represent him in the automobile accident case. That revelation was too much, even for me. Neither the son nor the mother had paid any fees in the criminal case.

The conduct of this mother and son in hiring the white lawyer for a case that a significant attorney fee could be gained while expecting the black lawyer to work for damn near free on the criminal matter was very prevalent. Some black people believe that African-American lawyers are not competent or capable to represent their interests in cases that have a significant dollar value attached to them. It is what I think Malcolm-X called self-hatred, one of the most significant by-products of hundreds of years of slavery. While I was crushed at the mother's action by that time, I developed a boilerplate letter, which in essence stated, *"there comes a time every relationship must end and we are at that point."* That letter, together with the criminal file, needless to say, was forwarded to the mother and son. I never heard from either again.

CHAPTER 13

Black Lackey

Black professionals in general have always endured a heavy burden of being considered of lesser intelligence than their white counterparts. In particular, black lawyers are thought of by many in the American judicial system as not being as competent as their white colleagues. I remember specifically growing up in South Carolina watching the Amos and Andy TV show. In the early 1950s, there were no TV shows that portrayed black characters in a positive light. Most of us, who were kids, were happy to see a black face on TV. The lawyer character, Calhoun, was depicted as significantly incompetent.

This lack of self-worth, I believe, is a direct consequence of slavery. To put differently, too many African-Americans still believe that we are incapable of rendering professional services to each other. While some historians and sociologists might say this is understandable, given the four hundred plus years of servitude enforced upon black people, it still has a devastating effect on us as a people. To this day, some white lawyers together with their, what I choose to call black lackeys, engage in every effort to take away from black lawyers, cases that have a potentially good fee attached to them. Here is how the scheme works. The black flunkies are sent to the client that has already retained an African-American lawyer. The bootlicker must denigrate the reputation, intelligence, and competence of the black lawyer, so as to convince the client that he or she will get an enormous settlement out of the case if they choose to hire the white lawyer after firing the black lawyer. If the client goes along with this nefarious scheme, the servant is given (normally) cash money by the Caucasian lawyer for having expropriated the case from the black lawyer. It is of no moment to the scoundrels that it is unethical for any lawyer to share a fee with a nonlawyer in regards to representation of a client. In some instances, I knew of occasions where the money was given to the modern-day boy before the case was even settled. There was one house-boy that was infamously known for executing this scheme with precision for the white lawyers.

Although this renowned bootlicker did significant damage to the financial well-being of a number of black lawyers, I think he achieved his ultimate aim. He is now a politician, an elected official, and a tool for those who control his very thoughts, his votes on various issues, and his livelihood. They own him.

I've always wondered what fiber one who was controlled by the dominant culture, was made of. I vowed early on in my professional career that I would not be submissive to any group because they had a misperception of my intelligence or capabilities due to the color of my skin. It became clear to me at an early age that there was a certain degree of confidence grounded in knowledge and preparation that a black person, professional or not, must have in order to compete with our white sisters and brothers in the legal profession in America.

In the area where I physically practice law, there was an unwritten rule that if a black lawyer had a good civil case from which he could make money, in terms of attorney fees, he or she was expected to refer that case to a white lawyer and the attorney fees would be divided equally among the two lawyers. That phenomenon reared its ugly head with me, in my practice, on more than one occasion. In one such instance, my client insisted, after many months of me exclusively representing her, that I associate this white lawyer on her case. It was truly and indeed a very good personal injury case worth mid six figures. I argued strongly and almost weekly with my client about her desire that I hire a white lawyer to help me with her case. Hell, I needed no help. It was a clear case of liability. In fact, about three months into the case, defense counsel for the insurance company told me that his company was going to pay the policy limits of about $500,000. I later found out that she was being encouraged by others, black persons, who were going to benefit by getting some under the table money from the white lawyer my client suggested we include.

The defense attorney asked me, "Why do you need to hire this other lawyer when I have told you I'm going to recommend that the insurance carrier pay the policy limits?" My retort to him was, "I was told by the client that I had to hire this other lawyer on the case." At that point in the case, I figured that half of a loaf, in terms of attorney fees, would be better than no fees.

After the case was settled, the ex-client, whom I had known practically all of her life, profusely apologized for what had occurred. She said she was confused, daily being influenced by these other persons and did not know what to do. I accepted her apology, forgave her, but never would I forget.

CHAPTER 14

"Fathead"

Early on in my practice, I was hired to represent a black defendant, James Harrison, in a criminal proceeding. He was charged with defrauding the Federal Government of a significant amount of money. There were two co-defendants. Both of them were Caucasian males. By that time, I suppose, I had developed a reputation as a punishing cross examiner of the prosecuting witnesses. The evidence in the case against these defendants were almost entirely documents. In the profession, a document-laden prosecution presented by the government is called a paper case. The presiding United States District Court judge was Charles Calhoun. He was referred to by some lawyers as *"fathead."* There was no neck between his head and his shoulders. His head, it appeared, sat on his shoulders. His head was very big. Based on my courtroom observations, Judge Calhoun's interaction with black defendants were short tempered and in some instances just downright mean. It was blatantly obvious that he had a significant amount of dislike for black people.

The two Caucasian defendants retained lawyers who were well-thought-of and high-powered. During the trial, our major disagreement, as lawyers, was there were a couple of government witnesses they thought should not be cross-examined.

I reasoned that this position was ludicrous. I rationalized that it would be very difficult to convince a jury that our clients, individually or collectively, were innocent if we could not create gaping holes in the Government's evidentiary presentation. I, almost summarily, disabused myself of the strategy of these witnesses being so locked and loaded so as to prevent cross examining them. I further realized that, on balance, I could not be exactly strategically aligned with the lawyers for the white defendants. The jurors would give the white defendants more benefit than doubt as opposed to the black defendant whom I represented.

Sticking with their strategy, none of the white lawyers cross-examined these, what I considered, essential government witnesses. However, when it became my turn to question these witnesses on behalf of my client, I unleashed withering attacks through cross-examination on the sufficiency of their paper evidence. I tried to systematically destroy every critical element in the documents referred to in their testimony. None of these government witnesses had any firsthand knowledge of the alleged fraud perpetrated by any of the defendants. It took about five days for the government to present its case. The government rested its case. That means that it had no more witnesses to call or evidence to present.

At this point in cases, the lawyer for the defendant is then given an opportunity to request or make a motion to the court for directed verdict. Essentially, the defendant represents to the court, by oral argument, that the government has not presented evidence sufficient to prove all of the elements of the criminal charge lodged against the defendant. After the government lawyer replies to the argument the defendant has made for a verdict, the judge is then obliged to make a ruling on the motion. The motion, arguments, and the judge's ruling are made outside of the presence of the jury.

United States District Court Judge Charles Calhoun began to make his rulings in open court by saying, "This case reminds me of a case I had when I first got out of law school where I represented this nigger boy." Perhaps realizing what he had said, the judge struck the gavel and stated, "The court is in recess for fifteen minutes." After he left the bench to go to his chambers, the lawyers representing the two white defendants rushed over to me and, almost in unison, said, "Now he didn't say what you thought he said, he said Nigra." My response was, "How in the F-- are you going to tell me what I heard. He said Nigger. I heard it and so did you." I could not understand the defensive posture that these other lawyers were taking regarding the obvious racist comment made by a United States District Court judge—from the bench for that matter. Given the unfairness that this judge had exhibited against the defendants up to this point in the trial, it would have been, in my opinion, to our communal advantage to request that this judge recuse himself from the case. Neither of the other lawyers, representing the white defendants, thought that was a good strategy. I was not interested in what they thought was best for their clients. My only interest was, at that point in the trial, to protect the rights of my client to get a fair trial. A judge that uses that or any racial epithet during the trial of a black defendant certainly cannot administer blind justice. I profusely argued with my client that I needed to make a motion for this judge to recuse himself and that was vital. At first, he agreed. Then he began to discuss what I wanted to do with the other defendants. Those defendants and their lawyers convinced him that a motion for recusal was not the proper course. No matter how much I pleaded with him on that day, he said he did not want to go down that road and would take his chances with this judge. I was livid, but had to compose myself so as to continue mounting a spirited defense for him against these charges.

About an hour later, the judge reconvened the trial. He ruled against the motions for directed verdict and proceeded forth with the trial as though nothing had occurred. I continued to try to convince my client that this judge was not going to be fair to him. He continued to resist my every attempt to make that motion for recusal. To this day, I was never presented with a rational reason as to why my client, a black man, would not let me make the motion for this judge to remove himself from his case. At some point before the end of the trial, I gained a degree of comfort and resigned myself to the thought of the consequences of this strategic decision was not a burden I would shoulder. The jury came back with a verdict of guilty against my client, and not guilty for one of the white defendants and a guilty verdict for the other white defendant. While I was troubled by the verdict, I lost very little sleep, if any, because of it. As my father would tell me while I was growing up, "A hard head breeds a soft ass." My client was sentenced to two years in prison. I was informed that *"fathead"* had a massive stroke while presiding in a later case. I was further informed that he suffered mightily and for a lengthy period of time before he was consumed by life's common denominator, death. Karma is a B---ch.

The use of the n-word was not unique to this criminal trial. What was different is that judge Calhoun used the n-word in open court. Other judges in the State of South Carolina and the South had used the n-word in open court. In 2003, Charleston County Magistrate Jim Suggs stated in open court, "There are four kinds of people in this world—black people, white people, rednecks and n-----s." Suggs was addressing a black defendant at a bond hearing. Although he was publicly reprimanded by the South Carolina Supreme Court, he was allowed to remain a judge. At the initial court appearance of the white supremacist Dylann Roof, whom had just murdered nine black parishioners while they were at Bible study, Suggs said the Roof family were also victims in this horrific crime. In no uncertain terms he said they did not ask to become a part of this tragedy and they need help too. Nine black people are dead and the killer's family needs help. Those statements in my opinion were a reflection of the empathy this judge held for the killer. If the family of Mr. Roof was not so steeped in racism, I doubt seriously whether Mr. Roof would have become the mass killer that he is. Roof did not raise himself. Those feelings he harbored towards black people and other minorities were nurtured in the home and community in which he grew up. No serious consequence other than a very short-lived public outcry was levied against Suggs. He still remains on the bench as a judge.

While use of the n-word is perhaps commonplace in private among some members of the judiciary, it rarely raises its atrocious head as it did in the case of Louisiana Judge Jessie LeBlanc. She used the term repeatedly in text messages to her lover Bruce Prejean, Chief Deputy for Assumption Parish in Louisiana. As I looked at those text messages, one of the conclusions that can be drawn was that the judge was upset because she believed that Prejean was having an affair with a black woman. Mind you, both Prejean and LeBlanc were married to other people. The direct quote from *The Advocate*, a local newspaper, is, "Among LeBlanc's racist comments in the text messages, she indicated that she had never been unfaithful to Prejean but in doing so also seemed to suggest her suspicions of Prejean's purported new affair were made even worse because it was, she believed, with a black woman: "At least I was NEVER unfaithful to you with ANYONE—much less a n----." When initially confronted with the text messages containing repeated racial epithets, LeBlanc refused to resign. Only after a press conference from the Governor calling on LeBlanc to relinquish her position as a judge, did she step down. Although not hearing cases, she still remains a judge in the Louisiana judicial system. This is 2021 folks. LeBlanc said she quit to *stop the madness.* Rhetorically, I ask how can anyone with LeBlanc's racial predisposition be impartial in meeting out justice? These revelations confirm my belief that equal justice before the law is rarely, if ever, available if you are black in America.

CHAPTER 15

The Dog Case

More than twenty years ago, I represented a Hispanic-American in what I considered to be a significantly non-sensical case. The only reason this man was being prosecuted was because he was not white. José Lopez was an American citizen from a South American country. He had a very pronounced Latin accent. One of José's friends, who was a legal alien, decided that he wanted to leave this country to go back to his native land. José's friend, Gonzales, had a dog. He did not have enough money to take the dog to South America with him. He gave the dog to José. This all occurred during the summer months. José, in transporting the dog from where Gonzales lived to his house, left the dog in his car with the windows down just enough so that adequate air could circulate through the car while he went into Walmart to secure some food items. The dog was in the car less than ten minutes. When he got back to his car from shopping at Walmart, there were four police cruisers with flashing lights surrounding his car. As José described what he encountered to me, it was as if he had committed murder or robbed a bank. Apparently after the police officers were able to discern his ethnicity, all guns were drawn and trained on him. He was immediately arrested and charged with cruelty to an animal. The dog was taken to the Charleston

County Animal Shelter. The law in South Carolina at that time, presented an exposure to two years in prison, if convicted.

José was a man of very modest means. He worked odd jobs, mostly doing carpentry to make ends meet. I would suspect that he made no more than $25,000 a year. He and his wife were very religious. He was the sole provider for his family: a wife and two small kids. When we initially met, it became clear to me that if he were convicted of this *alleged* crime, his family would be relegated to the public dole. I remember succinctly the thought that it would be disgraceful and disastrous for this entire family if their one and only breadwinner went to jail.

At that time, the push for stiffer penalties and making examples of persons thought to be cruel to animals was just gaining momentum. Now, let me hasten to add that I am all in favor of protecting animals from those who would abuse them. However, in this instance, in this case, I sense that there was a concerted effort to make an example out of José by imprisoning him. Up to that point, I don't have any recollection of anyone being imprisoned for cruelty to animals under the circumstances that constituted the facts of his case. And to this day, I firmly believe the only reason that the local Society for the Prevention of Cruelty to Animals (SPCA) leadership calculated that they would succeed in their attempt to send José away to prison was because he was of Hispanic descent. I was determined that I was going to do everything in my power, use every legal skill and courtroom oration, to make sure that didn't happen.

Before the case was called for trial, the prosecutor offered a plea of guilty in exchange for twelve months in prison. In my mind that offer was insane and forthrightly rejected. Having analyzed the dynamics of the efforts of the prosecutor, in conjunction with the local SPCA, I decided to take my chances with a jury. My thought process was that it would be easier to convince one of twelve members of the jury that José was not guilty. Pretrial negotiations resulting in the plea offer led me to conclude that a bench trial before the judge would undoubtedly result in José being found guilty and sentenced to prison. In a bench trial, the judge, he or she, is the trier of the facts and the law. In a jury trial, the judge can only inform the jury as to what the law is that would apply to the facts of the case. Then the jury decides the truth in regards to the facts of the case and renders a verdict.

In this American Judicial System, the notion is put forth that a defendant is tried before a jury of his or her peers. On the day that the jury was selected, I saw no one that looked obviously like a peer of José. In 1999, when this case was tried, it cost the county government $5,000 per day to operate a courtroom in which a jury trial was being conducted. This case was tried for three days. That cost did not include salaries for the prosecutor, as well as the police officers who testified. So, the prosecutorial arm of the county government, I'm sure with the significant encouragement from the local SPCA, was going to spend $6,000.00 plus per day to try and put this Hispanic man in jail.

I believe that while the assistant prosecutor assigned to try this case wanted to win to enhance his standing with his boss, he didn't necessarily want to see my client go to jail. During cross-examination of the state's witnesses in the trial, it became obvious to some members of the jury and to those in the courtroom that this case was being tried to placate the local SPCA. While on a break during the second day of the trial, one of the Circuit Court judges, who was no friend of mine, stopped me in the corridor of the courthouse and asked, "Why in the hell are they trying this case?" Unsure of his motives, I responded, "I don't have an answer." After the end of the first day of the trial, there was a buzz in the courthouse about what was later referred to as "the dog case." Testimony came out in the trial from SPCA employees that the dog was not injured. An SPCA worker testified that immediately after bringing the dog to the shelter, it was somewhat dehydrated. That was not a life-threatening condition.

Every day of the trial, the local President of the SPCA was in the courtroom. The prosecutor spent all three days putting up nonsensical and, in my opinion, unrelated evidence. At each turn, I made a valiant effort to discredit the evidentiary presentation. My client testified during the trial. The jury, at least some members, were impressed with his humility and honesty. He testified, among other things, that he had no intent to harm the dog and he was only trying to do his friend a favor by taking possession of the dog. When he was arrested by the police, he was on his way to his home. The purpose of the stop at Walmart was to get some food for the dog.

Anytime a prosecutor, who has all of the many resources of the State on his side in trying a case, does not secure a guilty verdict from the jury, that is considered a loss. The jury, being charged by the judge as to what the law was to apply to the facts of the case, began to deliberate. There were two "bubbas" on the jury. In legal circles, a bubba is a white man, who is usually a redneck, with a beer belly. When there is a black defendant, bubbas are the worst jurors.

Otherwise, the racial makeup of the jury was four blacks and seven whites, and I later discovered a woman was Hispanic, although I could not tell she was Hispanic when she was selected to sit on the jury. After nine hours, the jury was unable to reach a unanimous verdict. The judge brought the

jury back to the courtroom. He encouraged them to continue their deliberations in an attempt to reach a verdict. There
was nothing unusual about asking jurors to make an additional attempt to reach a verdict. My confidence that a guilty
verdict was not going to be reached by this jury was raised
significantly. After an additional two hours of deliberations,
the judge was informed by the jury that they were hopelessly
deadlocked and could not reach a verdict. He dismissed the
jury and thanked them for their service. The prosecutor and
the local SPCA representative were obviously very disappoint-
ed. The prosecutor informed all who would listen that the
case would be retried as soon as possible. I canvassed a couple
of the jury members after the trial. They were split eight to
four for a not guilty verdict.

The *"dog case"* was set for retrial some three weeks after the
first trial. The judge that was going to be presiding over the
retrial, routinely, wanted on early Monday morning, for the
prosecutors and the defense counsels to come to his chambers and inform him what kinds of cases were going to be
tried during the following week. Ours was the first case to
be tried, according to the prosecutor. Judge White asked the
prosecutor to explain the nature of the case. He informed the
judge that this was a case of alleged animal cruelty and that it
would take approximately three days to try the case. As if he
didn't hear what the prosecutor said the case was about, the
judge asked again, "What did you say about the facts of this
case?" The prosecutor repeated what he had said to the judge.
Judge White then asked, "Did the dog die?" The prosecutor
answered no. The judge further asked, "Was the dog significantly injured?" The prosecutor said somewhat. Judge White
unleashed a verbal barrage on this prosecutor that made me
feel bad for him. Not to quote verbatim what the judge said,

but essentially, he stated, *this case will not be tried in my courtroom under no circumstances and at no time. This is a waste of the court's resources and time.* He further stated that this case should have never been brought in the Court of General Sessions nor should this defendant have been charged under the felony statute. "This case belongs in Magistrate Court and that's where you are going to take it," he told the prosecutor. Judge White gave this prosecutor a vicious tongue lashing. Of course, all of that was music to my ears. Ultimately, my client was allowed to do five hours of community service. The case was dismissed. The only fee that I collected for this case was $750.00 paid by José's church.

CHAPTER 16

Excessive Fines

In an 1893 speech manuscript, Frederick Douglass talks about the convict leasing system that was put in place by southern states after the Civil War. This manuscript is found in the Library of Congress. In the speech contained in the manuscript, Douglas says, "Under the convict leasing system, the criminals are leased in bulk in their respective states, to whoever has the political ring, and that party, by paying a small sum to the State, sublets them in gangs to railroads and other corporations, and to plantations. The State throws off the entire responsibility of caring for her convicts, and turns them over into the hands of the lessee, whose only interest in them is, to secure for himself, what profits he can for their labor." Approximately ninety-five percent, if not more, of these convicts that were leased were black men. After the Civil War, southern states needed to regain control over the freed slaves, so that they could maintain a system of free labor. The Thirteenth Amendment to the United States Constitution was enacted by Congress after the Civil War. The amendment states, "Neither slavery nor involuntary servitude, except as punishment for crime where all of the party shall have been duly convicted, shall exist within the United States, or any place subject to their jurisdiction." The fatal flaw in the wording, "except as a punishment for crime whereof the party shall have been duly convicted", of that Amendment gave Southern states the legal right to re-enslave black people without consequence. Many aspects of the newly freed slaves' lives became criminalized by these laws passed by Southern state legislatures, county, and city governing bodies. These are known as "Black codes" and "pig laws." A favorite charge was vagrancy. Those codes gave the county Sheriff and local police the authority to arrest black persons for being vagrants (homeless). When they were found guilty, the sentence was a specific number of days of hard labor. After a person, almost exclusively black, was found guilty, the County Sheriff could and routinely did hire out the black prisoner to a white employer to work off their punishment. White people who were arrested and tried as vagrants were rarely, if ever, punished under the vagrancy laws. Instead, they were permitted to take an oath of poverty, which prevented confinement in a jail. There is no definitive number on the amount of the black persons that suffered the indignities embedded in the corrupt judicial system that enforced the black codes. I would suggest that there were millions of people of color who were physically and emotionally mangled in the claws of that depraved system.

Some have stated that this ungodly system ended in 1941. I beg to differ. The system retooled itself and is alive and well when it comes to black people. The money collected from the leasing of black persons convicted under this dastard, black-code system, went directly to the coffers of the Sheriff or the county government. While the practice of direct leasing of prisoners to add to the budget of the Sheriff or municipalities may have changed, the mechanism inherent in its purpose to garner money for city and county government, has not. The black codes have resurfaced by way of excessive fines for violations, misdemeanors or ordinances levied against black and poor people. Those fines and court costs go directly to supplementing the budgets of city and county governments. Without fail these fines and court costs fall disproportionately on people of color. A visit to any criminal court on any day will reveal that approximately seventy percent of the people there who are defendants are black. That is true in spite of the fact that African-Americans make up less than fifteen percent of the general population.

The Eighth Amendment to the United States Constitution forbids excessive fines. Most states have a parallel provision in their Constitution. I was always amazed that most lawyers would evade making the excessive fine argument before courts on behalf of their clients. I believe that in not making the argument the client was being subjected to additional punishment above and beyond what the ordinance or misdemeanor required. I made that argument every chance I could. The practical problem with making the excessive fine argument was that you were very unlikely to win. I made the argument for the purpose of protecting the record if the case was appealed. Most city or county magistrate judges were appointed. Those who appointed them could, at the end of their term, remove them. The city court judge knows that, in large measures, his or her job is to impose these excessive fines to build up the city's budget. This method of collecting money from people, usually more than eighty percent black, is much easier than imposing a tax on all residents and businesses within its borders. For whom among us could credibly argue that these fines and excessive fees are nothing more than a tax to augment city and county budgets.

Across America, as much as forty percent of many towns and cities (whose law enforcement officers issue traffic tickets for violations of local ordinances) use the fines collected to support their budgets. This is a practice that most heavily harms minorities and the poor. Here is how it works. Police officers are encouraged, if not required by their superiors, to issue a minimum amount of tickets on a daily basis. That figure could range anywhere from four to ten. The average fine that has to be paid because of the ticket is approximately $200. That amount does not include fees and other court costs that must be paid.

Before 1971, many municipalities would automatically impose a jail sentence on a defendant who could not pay the fine. In *Tate v. Short*, the United States Supreme Court held that the equal protection clause of the Fourteenth Amendment *"prohibits the state from imposing a fine as a sentence and then automatically converting it into a jail term solely because the defendant is indigent and cannot forthwith pay the fine in full."* After 1971, local governments did not stop imposing excessive fines on people of color for traffic violations. I have no recollection of being at a city court to represent a client on a traffic ticket where less than seventy percent of the persons who were issued tickets were African-Americans. This fact is particularly telling of the racially motivated conduct of the police force and court system because blacks only make up about fifteen percent of the general population of these United States. I remember on many occasions internalizing the thought that apparently white people don't violate the traffic laws.

A couple of instances clearly isolate themselves in my mind. I was representing a black client in the city of North Charleston's Municipal Court. The client was charged with violation of a city ordinance for a minor amount of debris in her front yard. More than eighty percent of the persons who were summoned to appear before this court on that day were black. As I sat waiting for my client's case to be heard in front of the judge, every black defendant was fined. No time was given to pay the fine. It had to be paid on that day. No white person was treated the same. They were given up to thirty days to pay their fines. The white Judge's conduct was overwhelmingly racist. All who were in the courtroom knew that to be true. When my client's case was called to be heard, I decided that I was going to challenge this maniacal son of a bitch.

Immediately, I informed the judge that we wanted a jury trial and that I was appalled that all of the black defendants whose cases were called before mine were treated monumentally unfairly. He was probably not shocked at my verbal attack on his integrity. I had battled, mightily, with him in many other criminal cases. And because of our combative history, he further understood that I was not going to back down. I was determined that there would be no fines levied against my client for this alleged violation of a city ordinance. The case was favorably disposed of with a warning citation, but the City of North Charleston's action through this judge leads me to conclude that this collection of excessive fines and fees against the people, usually black, who could least afford it, was a common practice. I wished that I could have represented all of those previous black defendants that came before him on that day. Once again, I witnessed black people being on the receiving end of a blatantly racist judicial system.

I have had my own personal encounters with these kinds of traffic stops. One day I was traveling from Charleston, South Carolina to Atlanta, Georgia. Instead of using the interstate, I decided to travel what is commonly referred to as two-lane state highways. That route led me through a number of small towns in South Carolina. One such town was Springfield. Springfield had two police officers. On the day of my travel, I saw the blue lights on a SUV behind me. There was a car in front of me, so, I nonchalantly thought the blue lights had to be directed at the car that I was following. I slowed down my vehicle to let the SUV with the blue lights flashing go around me. As I peered through my rearview mirror, it became clear that he was stopping me. I pulled over to the side of the road and the officer stopped the SUV behind me with blue lights continuously flashing. He got out of his car and came to the passenger side of my vehicle. As he was approaching, I saw out of the mirror on the passenger side that he had unstrapped his revolver. Remaining calm, he asked me, after I rolled down the window, "Do you know why I stopped you?" I told him in a rather matter of fact tone, "No." While I was not fearful for my life at that moment, perhaps I should have been. He asked for my driver's license and registration and I gave both items to him. He went to his car and wrote a ticket for speeding. He got out of his car, came to the driver side window, and hand-ed me the ticket. All the while I was very pleasant with him because I knew that I was not speeding and that this ticket would be challenged. So, the officer proceeded to tell me that the fine would be $150, and I could mail that to the court ad-dress on the ticket and would not have to appear in court. My response to him was, "Don't I have a constitutional right to a jury trial?" He reluctantly told me that I did, but said very few people requested that. Feeling compelled to deflate the ego of this redneck dawning the police uniform, I informed him that I was an attorney and that I would be requesting a jury trial. It was at that moment that I saw disgust in his face. It was now red. I asked if it were anything else that he needed to inform me of. He said "No," got in his SUV, and made a vicious U-turn. He was clearly angry. The story does not end there.

I requested a jury trial from the town of Springfield, in writing on my letterhead. About two weeks later, I received a telephone call from the Municipal Court judge for Springfield, South Carolina. His exact words to me were, "Now Mr. Brown, I know you may not agree with me, but, ah, we met and we decided we are going to dismiss this case. Is that alright with you Mr. Brown?" Of course, I said yes. Not leaving anything to chance, I confirm the tenor of my telephone conversation with this judge in writing, again on my letterhead.

The next encounter with a small-town police officer—who needed to write a ticket to meet his quota for the month—occurred in Yemassee, South Carolina. While driving south on Highway 17 to Savannah, Georgia, I was stopped by a Yemassee police officer. The same nonsense occurred, "Do you know why you're being stopped?" I really did not because I was certainly not speeding. I told him no I did not know why I was being stopped. He went to his car after getting my driver's license and car registration…came back with the ticket for speeding. The police officer told me that I did not have to appear before the Municipal Court judge and that I could mail in the fine of $175 for the ticket. Here we have another redneck police officer believing that he could tell me anything and I would believe it. I told him that I would be exercising my right to a jury trial. It looked to me like he became depressed. I requested a jury trial in writing, again, on my attorney's letterhead. When one requests a jury trial, the municipality must give you a date and time to appear before that court for the jury trial. I never got any correspondence from this town telling me when I needed to appear for the jury trial. For any defendant, this is fundamental fairness.

This little town was so desperate for the fine, the Yemassee Municipal Court judge conducted the trial in my absence.

About a month after the trial date, I received a letter from them indicating the fine had increased significantly because

I didn't show up for trial. After having an extensive telephone conversation with the Municipal Court judge, I faxed to his office a copy of the letter on my office letterhead where I previously requested a jury trial. That didn't matter to him, apparently, because he still insisted that I needed to pay the fine. I told him that if this guilty verdict was not removed from my record, I would be bringing a lawsuit against the town of Yamasee in a court of competent jurisdiction. The finding of guilty was expunged from my record. To this day, I have yet to receive a notice from the town of Yemassee informing me as to when a jury trial is going to occur. I often wonder how many black and impoverished persons are put through this grinding and unfair mechanism designed solely for the purpose of supporting the budget of these cities and towns.

If the person that received the ticket does not show up for court or cannot pay the fine in a timely fashion, their license is usually suspended. That leads to a multiplicity of other serious consequences. "The consequences of criminalization of poverty are not only harmful—they are far-reaching," said Attorney General Loretta Lynch in a news release. "They not only affect an individual's ability to support their family, but also contribute to an erosion of our faith in government." I don't have to be as nice as the former Attorney General Loretta Lynch. For when it comes to having faith in any institution conceived by people of ill-will, including local governments, for the purpose of rendering fair and equal justice to black people, I need only point to four hundred years of history.

CHAPTER 17

Rape Case

Growing up on Wadmalaw Island as a black male was extremely trying when it came to association with the few white people, especially white women, that I came in contact with. White men were viciously against any form of integration in the daytime. At night, however, there was another story. Many of them (as Thomas Jefferson and men of his day) believed they had the right to have sex, at their pleasure, with any black woman they deemed desirable.

I grew up with many children who, by the coloration of the skin, were grandchildren or children of white men. There was never any social outcry when these white scoundrels fathered, but offered no support to the well-being of, their half black offspring. In the early sixties, a radio talk show host by the name of David Joiner, a minister, railed almost daily against the segregationist United States Senator from South Carolina, Strom Thurmond. Strom Thurmond fathered a child with Carrie Butler, a fifteen-year-old black female domestic worker who was employed by his family. Thurmond was twenty-two years old. Segregation was convenient only when it was convenient. There was no arrest warrant issued for Strom Thurmond's statutory rape. He would not have had the alleged defense Jefferson had in regards to impregnating a fifteen-year-old. Ms. Butler was not Strom Thurmond's property, as many historians claimed Sally Hemming was in defending Thomas Jefferson's action.

Black men, on the other hand, were lynched and murdered for looking the wrong way at white women. And in many instances, the white women were attracted to and had intimate relationships with black men. However, those relationships had to be kept secret. Not being clandestine would almost surely result in being arrested and possibly death, under the vestiges of the Black codes. Generally, the Black codes and Jim Crow laws were a series of laws passed by Southern states legislatures after the Civil War and the Reconstruction era designed to keep black people socially and economically enslaved. The overarching purpose was to maintain white supremacy. With extremely rare exceptions, the white women were never penalized. Never were they, even remotely, in any criminal jeopardy. They were always portrayed as the unwilling victims. It matters not that in most, if not all, of these sexual interactions were consensual. The diabolical intent of the white power structure and law enforcement was that they had to keep these Negroes in their place. Black men cannot be allowed to be engaged sexually with "pristine" white women. If the white woman was married to a white man and it was discovered that she had a sexual liaison with a black man, that would almost always bring about a criminal charge of rape. I guess that was a step up from being lynched.

In the early eighties, I participated in the defense of a black man who was charged with allegedly raping a white woman. Charles Hanson and Rebecca Howell had an ongoing sexual relationship for a period in excess of five years. He was black and she was white. These two people had a genuine love for each other. Mrs. Howell's husband found out about the intimate relationship. In this small rural county, Mr. Howell was

a man of moderate means. There was some gossip about Howell's wife, Rebecca, sleeping with a black man. As far as beauty
is defined by Nordic standards, Rebecca was a good-looking
woman. My client was attractively tall, light-skinned and
probably a product of nighttime integration. Nonetheless, he
was identified as black. I never completely understood how
they got to the point of being lovers. Mr. Hanson said they
initially met at the gas pump at a local convenience store.
He said there was an instant attraction and they exchanged
telephone numbers. I hesitate to call their situation a tryst.
For, from my many conversations with Mr. Hanson, I got the
distinct impression that there was a genuine emotional connection between him and Mrs. Howell. Many of their rendez-
vous would be at hotels in an adjoining town. While he was
able to provide me with some receipts, those alone would not
prove Mrs. Howell was at the hotels with him.

Historically, a black man in American culture, particularly in the South, having consensual sex with a white woman
could and did reap fatal consequences. This case was approximately thirty years removed from the murder of Emmett Till
for looking inappropriately at a white woman in Mississippi.
In 1951, Matt Ingram, a black sharecropper in Yanceyville,
North Carolina was convicted of assault with intent to rape
of a seventeen-year-old white girl name Willa Jean Boswell
**just because he looked at her in a manner that she did not
like. Both of those cases were because of the Jim Crow error's
"reckless eyeballing laws." Admittedly, my client Mr. Hanson
was doing much more than recklessly eyeballing Ms. Howell.
And it appeared that both of them were enjoying the intimacy
they shared. Of course, as was usual, after Mr. Howell discovered and Mrs. Howell confessed to the sexual connection with
my client, she was forced by her husband to file a complaint

with the law enforcement that Mr. Hanson had raped her. So tragic was this state of affairs. It could not be admitted that Mrs. Howell had consensual sexual intercourse, on many occasions, with this black man. In the minds of many white people, the Howell's family name would be forever shamed and disgraced.

Despite the historical backdrop of black men being summarily convicted, by all-white juries, and in some instances executed for alleged rape of white women, I was prepared to roll the dice for Mr. Hanson. Given the racial makeup of that county, I did not believe the prosecutor would be able to strike all of the blacks from the jury panel. Thus, I believed that we could get, perhaps, one or two strong black people on the jury. It would only take one of those twelve to hang the jury. Because of all the salacious details that would be brought forward in this trial, there would probably be less appetite by the prosecutor to engage in a second trial if the first trial ended without a guilty verdict. But that was a two-edged sword. Those details could also enrage the white establishment to demand a second trial if the first trial ended with a hung jury. I did not believe that Mrs. Howell would be believable in testifying that she did not consent to being sexually intimate with Mr. Hanson on many occasions. Hell, my calculations were that it would be difficult for her to convince a black juror that all of the numerous times she had sex with Mr. Hanson was rape. This case was more about enforcing the black codes and protecting the honor of a white man more than anything else. He, Mr. Howell, was, I'm sure, ridiculed by his peers because his wife had slept with a black man. As per usual, the county law enforcement and judicial system would be used to punish the black man with imprisonment and therefore re-dignify Mr. Howell's name. Rhetorically, *why did this black man feel that he was good enough to go to bed and make love to my white wife?* The prosecutor also ran a risk of losing this case. I surmised that he believed that Mrs. Howell would not present to a jury as a convincing victim.

This entire charade, passing itself off as justice, was a mechanism designed from its inception, to maintain the dominance of being white. Black people, especially black men, had to be kept in their place. The dignity of Mr. Howell was damaged by his wife having a long-standing sexual affair with Mr. Hanson. His rights as a white man had to be vindicated through this state-supported system of judicial racism.

While I was not the lead attorney defending Mr. Hanson, I was determined to make my voice heard on the strategic approach that we should take in trying this institutionalized racist action masked as a rape criminal case. The three lawyers defending Mr. Hanson were black. All of the prosecutors were white. It would have been a double whammy if the prosecutor lost this case and that loss came at the hands of black attorneys. Such a loss would be looked at by the white community as a substantial dent in this prosecutor's armor and white superiority. As usual, there was a strong undercurrent of gossip in the community about this so-called rape of Mrs. Howell by Mr. Hanson. Most of the black people that we talked to knew of the sexual relationship between Howell and Hanson. I'm not sure what the white community thought, but my suspicion was that some of them also knew of the sexual liaison between these two individuals.

Before the trial, the prosecutor presented what he called, *"a good deal."* If Mr. Hanson pled guilty to rape, he would recommend ten years imprisonment. If a jury found Mr. Hanson guilty, the trial judge would have given him the maximum of twenty-five years. My thoughts were that the prosecutor was not confident that a jury would return a guilty verdict after analyzing the facts of this case. The defense team huddled with the defendant for about fifteen minutes before responding to the prosecutor's offer. I was vehemently against Mr. Hanson taking this deal. If, as I argued, the prosecutor knew that this was a slam dunk case he would not have offered anything. I loudly voiced to the team that the prosecutor was very unsure of what Mrs. Howell would say on the witness stand. My gut instinct was that Mrs. Howell was going to admit that her sexual encounters with Mr. Hanson were voluntary.

During these plea negotiations, I was forced to take a bathroom break. On my way back from the bathroom, I was stopped in the hallway by an elderly black gentleman, whose name I do not remember. He said he wanted to ask a legal question. He and I were facing each other. As we began to converse, I saw the alleged victim, Ms. Howell, and her husband sitting on a bench in the same corridor. As the older gentleman began to talk, I visually became irreversibly focused on the demeanor of Mrs. Howell. She did not look enraged or as a female that had been sexually violated. I remembered that the law enforcement reports made no mention of bruises being on her body as a result of the so-called rape. She did look distressed, but not because of being sexually assaulted by my client. For a brief moment, our eyes met. As she looked at me, Mrs. Howell shook her head from side to side. Her outward behavior on that day conveyed to me the distinct impression that she did not want to be involved with sending our client, her lover, to jail. There was no comforting of her by Mr. Howell. She was being forced to complain that she was a victim of a sexual assault by my client. He was on one end of the bench and she was on the other. For the entire time of my observing both of them, neither one spoke a word to the other. I concluded that there was genuine caring by Mrs. Howell for Mr. Hanson that culminated in sexual intimacy between them. Mr. Howell's mannerism was one that displayed the thought, *I'm going to teach this nigger that he cannot have sexual intercourse with a white woman, especially my wife. I must have my pride and white privilege restored.*

I heard very little of what the black gentleman in the hall said to me. When he asked me what I thought of what he told me, I kind of stuttered and gave him my card. I told him to call my office and make an appointment so that we can further discuss this matter in more detail.

Armed with what I perceived as a new and vital insight into the prosecution's case, I rushed back to my colleagues and the client to inform them of my impressions. At that point, I was significantly convinced that our defense team could totally exonerate Mr. Hanson. I was prepared to make this a bad day for the prosecution.

Mr. Hanson however, was afraid and rightfully so. If he were found guilty by a jury, he was going to jail for twenty-five years. The other thing that came to my mind was that our client did not want his lover facing the kind of cross-examination that would occur if Mrs. Hanson took the witness stand to testify. Our counter offer to the prosecutor was that Mr. Hanson would plead guilty to a lesser included offense, but there would be no jail time, only probation. I felt very uncomfortable with that counter offer, but the ultimate decision was that of the client, Mr. Hanson. The prosecutor then came back with an offer of five years maximum to a guilty plea of rape. The prosecutor dropping the ten years to five years in prison, sustained my belief that Mrs. Howell was not prepared to go to the witness stand and testify in the definitive manner that he would need in order to get a conviction. While we were not there yet, I felt confident at that point that we would be able to secure for Mr. Hanson, complete vindication. But yet again, Mr. Hanson was very skittish about going to trial fearing a guilty verdict and a long prison sentence.

I was more intense now in arguing that we could win this case before a jury if Mr. Hanson would allow us to go to trial. I was convinced of that because the list of potential jurors provided to us before the trial was thirty-eight percent black. Statistically, that meant that we could get possibly four jurors seated on a twelve-person jury. I believe that when the facts of the case were laid out before a jury, no black person would vote to convict Mr. Hanson of rape. At a very minimum, I thought we could get a hung jury. But at the insistence of Mr. Hanson, we continued to negotiate to get a better plea deal. In my opinion, this case was all about trying to restore the good name of Mr. Howell in that a guilty verdict would prove to the white community that his wife had not voluntarily had sex with Mr. Hanson, but was forced to against her will. The entire phenomenon was such an absurd event, but nonetheless real with potentially devastating consequences for Mr. Hanson.

While this judge was usually very insistent on starting criminal cases for trial in a timely manner, there was no communication from his chambers that he wanted the trial to start. It was close to twelve o'clock and we were still negotiating with the Solicitor's office about a possible plea deal. That led me to conclude that the judge had wind of the facts of the case and perhaps wanted a resolution to occur other than by a full-blown trial. I thought it was time for us to call the prosecutor's bluff. We would tell him that we wanted nothing other than a full-blown trial. Let a jury of Mr. Hanson's peers decide whether he had raped Mrs. Howell.

After much arguing with the client and the other two members of the defense team, we presented our second counter offer to the prosecutor. Within less than fifteen minutes, the prosecutor presented a new plea deal which was a lesser included offense to the rape charge. At that point, I was thoroughly persuaded that the prosecutor was fearful of losing this case before a jury. However, our client did not share my enthusiasm or belief. The one year that was offered by the prosecutor was apparently music to our client's ear. He was truly fearful of prison. Although I remained steadfast in trying this case before a jury, our client decided to take the one-year deal.

As I reflect back on the factual underpinnings of this case, it was yet another tragedy perpetrated against a black man for having consensual sex with a white woman. I could not fault him for taking the plea deal. I made a pack from that day forward with my inner soul, that I would do everything humanly possible to dismantle this system of imprisoning black men for having consensual sex with white women. And at the end of that ignominious day, I thought of the centuries of rape and debauchery committed by the plantation owners and the overseers and the deranged white men against black women without penalty, my heart became, and still is, hardened. From that I drew strength to continue to pursue some form of justice in a patently unjust judicial system.

I had no further opportunity to legally represent Mr. Hanson again. I did not maintain contact with him. Some years later, being in the same courthouse on another criminal matter, I was approached by a black Sheriff's Deputy who asked me if I were one of the lawyers who represented Mr. Hanson. Of course, I told him yes. During the course of our conversation, he too expressed the hypocrisy of the whole process.

While I have no personal knowledge of this, the Deputy told me that Mrs. Howell left Mr. Howell and began living with Mr. Hanson within two months after he was released from prison. I don't know that this constitutes a happy ending, but it was an ending.

CHAPTER 18

Roll Call

Roll call is a system that was designed to make sure persons that had been charged, criminally, were still within the jurisdictional limit of the court. When I first started practicing law, roll call occurred on Monday mornings. Later on, the Prosecutor's Office moved the roll call day of the appearance to Fridays. It was always a significant struggle for me to maintain silence about the disproportionate number of people of color having to appear at roll call. In more than seventy-five percent of the counties in which I practiced, ninety percent of the defendants attending roll call were African-Americans. I often imagine that if an alien from another planet appeared at a roll call, they could easily conclude that only black people were charged with the commission of crimes. It was as if white people never violated the criminal laws. I harken back to the comedian Richard Pryor when during one of his performances, he retorted that he went down to the courthouse looking for justice and found "just us." African-Americans made up, at best, fifteen percent of the general population, but as much as eighty-five percent of the criminal defendants. What's wrong with that picture? Sometimes I felt so disgusted at the obvious injustice, it would become almost overwhelming. At those moments, I would reach into the most inner recesses of my being, to find the strength to continue the fight against the systematic degradation of black people. What was always so shocking to me, although it should not have been, was the ease with which the Caucasian participants: prosecutors, law enforcement, and judges operated this assembly-line mechanism of injustice towards black people.

It matters not to most of them, that you were in large measures, more equipped intellectually than they were. In one instance, the prosecutor whom I had played golf with repeatedly called me *"nigger."* I was negotiating with him telephonically about a possible plea deal for one of my clients. We both were on speakerphone. There were no harsh words between us during the negotiations. At least in my mind, I thought we were rather pleasant with one another. We didn't reach an agreement and in ending the conversation he said, "Ed, I'll talk to you later, I have another call." I didn't hang up the telephone and he kept talking as though he thought I had. While I don't know who was in the office with him, he said out loud, presumably to someone, "Can you believe that nigger is asking me to dismiss this case because of some constitutional bullshit. He's out of his nigger ass mine if he thinks that's going to happen." I remember being extremely angry. I thought about calling him back immediately and telling him I heard what he had said. But a calming peace cerebrally descended on me. My objective would now be how to use that disgusting utterance to the benefit of my client. I composed of verbatim statement of what I remembered him saying.

The next time I saw this prosecutor was at roll call. My client and I went there front and center. After the roll call, I pulled the prosecutor aside and told him I needed to talk with him. To this day, I don't know whether he was an avowed racist, but I deducted from my previous encounters with him, especially on the golf course, that he probably would not want to be called or be reported as a racist. I told him I had a document I wanted him to look at. I handed him a verbatim statement of what he said after he thought I was no longer on the telephone. After reading my sworn Affidavit, his eyes conveyed to me certain submissiveness. It was as if he thought that my Affidavit was going to be the basis for reporting him to the bar. I had no thought of traveling that path, for it would have been an effort in futility. But he didn't know that. He dashed away from my presence and in leaving, said nothing. The next day he called my office and said the case against my client would be dismissed. I haven't seen or heard from him since. That was more than fifteen years ago.

There are some who will read this and say I should have reported him to the bar. However, nothing would come of that effort. Having analyzed the pros and cons of that kind of course of conduct, it became more sensible for me to take the small victory of having the case dismissed against my client. Incidentally, he should have never been charged criminally with anything.

.

CHAPTER 19

Court Martials

There was somewhat of a strong appreciation for military service in the Wadmalaw Island Community. As a young lad, I remember the military being used as a vehicle to leave Wadmalaw Island, South Carolina. However, I have no distinct recollection of any black servicemen or women being given any respect that was deserving of a person serving their country by white people on Wadmalaw Island or anywhere else. When on leave from the post, in uniform, out of uniform, or carrying out daily assignments, black military service persons received no respite from the vestiges of slavery. In fact, a cursory inspection of the history of the treatment of black persons laying their lives on the line for the freedom in this country would reveal that discrimination in the military is just as, if not more, rampant than discrimination in America in general. The military is a mere extension of American society. The chronicles composing the history of this country are littered with murderous treatment of black servicemen, in or out of uniform, by civil authorities. In an article written by Peter C. Baker, November 27, 2016, for the *New Yorker* Magazine, the following quote from Bryan Stevenson, the founder and director of the Equal Justice Initiative is found, "We do so much in this country to celebrate and honor folks who risk their lives on the battlefield…" Stevenson further stated, "But we don't remember that black veterans were more likely to be attacked for their service than honored for it." The article further reads, "To be a soldier is to receive training in weapons, in organizations, in tactics: the skills of self-assertion. It is also to lay claim to the reverence that America sets aside for its former warriors. For these reasons, the return home of black soldiers after war has infuriated and terrified white America, setting the stage for reactionary aggression."

In 1940, the official U.S. military policy was, "*Officers for Negro units might be Negro or white.… Negro officers were to be chosen and trained according to the same standards as white officers and, preferably, trained in the same schools. Negro officers were to serve only with Negro units.… **and should command Negro troops only.**"*

In 1943, the following anonymous letter from a black soldier was sent to the late black Congressman Adam Clayton Powell of New York:

> "On August 31st 1943 a white private told a Negro Officer who had reprimanded him for not observing the ordinary military courtesy of a salute, if you would take your clothes off and lay them on the ground I would salute them but I wouldn't salute anything that looks like you. The Officer called a Captain and told him of the incident. In the presence of the private, the Captain said, 'Well Lieutenant, what do you want me to do about it?" The Officer reported the matter to the major under whom he was serving immediately. The Major advised, "I wouldn't make an issue of the incident if I were you.' The Officer

insisted on preferring a charge against the soldier. He was transferred from the post three days later."

This attitude of superiority has not progressed very far from its origin.

Admittedly, President Harry S. Truman did, by executive order, end segregation in the military in the late 1940s. And I'm not thoroughly convinced that the ending of segregation was moved by much other than the financial burden that would have had to be borne by a segregated military. Very little credence, if any, can be given to the idea that Truman's executive order changed many hearts. The disproportionate disciplining of black servicemembers in all the military branches are frightening. Black Marines are 2.6 times more likely to be found guilty in a general court-martial than their white counterparts. Black airmen are seventy-one percent more likely than their white counterparts to face court-martialed or non-judicial punishment. In the Army, black soldiers are sixty-one percent more likely to be court-martialed than white soldiers. For the Navy, that number is forty-one percent These statistics, to some, may be astounding because blacks in the 1980s made up around thirty percent of the military services. And perhaps, one should be aghast at these statistics given, and how history clearly documents that black men and women have, with a religious fervor, given their lives for the United States of America. It cannot be credibly argued that the branches of the military are unaware of these disproportionate numbers in regards to black soldiers. In a recent statement, Retired Col. Don Christensen, the President of the group Protect Our Defenders and former chief prosecutor of the Air Force, claimed that military leaders are and have been aware of the racial disparity in the disciplining of minority military members and have done nothing to address it. Col. Christensen further states, "Top brass has also vigor-ously opposed any suggestion that the commander-controlled justice system is hindered by conflicts of interest or bias and has gone to great lengths to tout the fairness of the system. However, the military's own data raises serious challenges to the idea that the system in its current form is capable of deliver-ing impartial justice." Those statements were made by Lt. Col. Christensen in 2017. Imagine what the military justice system did to black service members in the early 1980s and before.

I have represented a number of black servicemen during my forty-two-year tenure as a lawyer. There is one case where vicious injustices were levied against a black soldier. Nothing in the military records would convey the remote notion that the soldier did not love this country and relish being in the military. He was prepared to give his life to preserve its free-dom. However, the country, in general, and his command in particular, had no such love or appreciation for him.

In the early 1990s, Jack Johnson II was an enlisted seaman first class stationed aboard a ship at the Charleston military base. His basic training records revealed that he was a perfect fit for the Navy. He never had any issues following orders. He never went to Captain's mast. He did his job. His flaw however, was that he developed romantic feelings for a white female shipmate. Here again was the treacherous phenome-non of intimacy between a black man and a white woman. It was as if the words of many colonies and state legislature—rising from their archives—that black men having this lustful desire for sex with white American women must be violently suppressed. From the first day that African men touched the shores of this continent, white men have had this imaginary and insatiable fear about black men having sex with their wives, sisters, mothers and daughters.

Mr. Johnson's white Chief Petty Officer ordered him to come to his office. Upon arriving, he was greeted by Naval Investigative Service. My client was informed by the investigators that a rape had occurred on a ship and he was identified as the rapist. Without giving him time to digest the allegations, the investigators immediately began to try to get him to confess that he had raped his white female shipmate. They told him that he was positively identified by others as having been in the berthing quarters where the rape occurred. My client denied having raped anyone. When the shipmate's name was revealed to Mr. Johnson, he did admit to having a sexual relationship with her. He never wavered, despite the lies being told to him by the investigators in their efforts to get him to admit to something he did not do. This process continued on for more than three hours. I suspect that the investigators, two white men, became frustrated that my client would not confess. But that did not stop their efforts to try to extract a confession from him. They then escorted him off the ship to their headquarters on the base. Once there, the interrogation began anew and continued for an additional five hours. He was told by the investigators that they had done a rape vitullo kit and found black pubic hairs in the vaginal area of the alleged victim. It later turned out that this was a gigantic lie.

Lying to a suspect for the purpose of getting him to admit guilt is a perfectly legal investigative technique. Mr. Johnson repeated that he had numerous consensual sexual encounters with the white female shipmate at a friend's apartment off of the Naval Base. These two investigators employed every trick, lie, and deceptive tactic for the sole purpose of coercing a confession from Mr. Johnson. Much to their chagrin, he confessed to nothing other than having a sexual relationship with this white female shipmate. Interestingly, he was never told the date the alleged rape occurred. He later informed me, about four days before he was summoned to the Chief Petty officer's office that he had met and had sexual intercourse with the white female shipmate at a hotel near the Naval Base.

Jack Johnson, the father, told me during multiple face-to-face interviews, that his son loved the Navy. While growing up, his son always spoke of wanting to join the Navy. At Christmastime, the father would buy his son toys that were symbolic of the Navy. One Christmas, at the age of ten, the son insisted on his parents buying him a Navy uniform.

I found nothing particularly attractive about the physical features of the white female shipmate that Mr. Johnson was accused of raping. On a Navy ship, the berthing quarters are very close. From my interview with Mr. Johnson, I learned he had in fact had a sexual relationship with this white female shipmate. However, none of the intimacy occurred on the ship. Generally speaking, the allegation was that while this female was sleeping in her berthing bunk, Mr. Johnson allegedly crawled in the bed with this shipmate and had sex with her against her will. Whenever there is a rape, good investigative techniques require that the victim be taken to a health care provider so that a rape Vitullo kit can be secured. That was done in this case. The results were astonishing and logically convinced me that the Navy would not move forth with this prosecution. There were no pubic hairs of any African-American males to be found in the vaginal area of the white shipmate. There were pubic hairs from an unidentified white male. So, I thought, what is the problem? The DNA revealed that Mr. Johnson had sexual intercourse with the shipmate. However, the date and time of the intercourse could not be determined from the DNA. Certainly, at least as I was able to surmise, the white female shipmate had other sexual partner(s) than Mr. Johnson.

Couple that with the fact that this rape allegedly occurred on the ship while the female shipmate was in her berth where other females were also in their beds in the berthing area. I had never been on a military ship before. Therefore, I had no visual perception of what a berthing quarter looked like. One of the things I've always done to prepare in criminal cases is to do a personal inspection of the scene where the alleged crime occurred. I requested and was granted permission to visit the ship and more specifically the berthing area where this alleged rape supposedly took place. The closeness of the sleeping quarters on this vessel was such that it would have been impossible for my client to enter the quarters, rape this female shipmate, and go unnoticed. The sleeping area was within a compartment that had three bunk beds stacked on top of each other with about twenty-four to thirty inches vertically between the bed. The hallway was about three feet wide. The beds lined both sides of the compartment. The Navy produced no witnesses that were able to validate the female shipmate's account of the alleged rape. Other than the semen found in the vaginal cavity of the white female shipmate, no evidence connected my client to this woman on the day of the alleged rape.

I was thoroughly convinced that the Navy's prosecutor, whom I had not met in person, would dismiss this case given the lack of credible evidence against my client. Telephonically, the prosecutor did not appear to be overly anxious to try this case. Between the time of the first face-to-face meeting and the last telephone conversation, the prosecutor's position change 180 degrees. Later in the discovery process, he was much more aggressive, asserting that the Navy had to maintain good order. Over the course of those few months, when we first talked and the latter in-person meeting, I could tell something or someone was forcing him to prosecute this case.

This prosecutor was slightly built with red hair. His mustache was neatly trimmed. He was a marine. Every one of his mannerisms conveyed the notion that he believed he was more competent than I and that I should be grateful for whatever plea offer he would make.

In a military court martial, unlike a civilian criminal trial, the jury verdict need not be unanimous. A majority of the jurors can convict a fellow service member on criminal charges. The judge is usually an officer in the military with a law degree.

In sizing up the military judge, he appeared to be a man steeped in military traditions. In some banter talk while in his chambers, it was revealed that he was in his late forties or early fifties. I did not expect that I or my client would get any benefit of the doubt in regard to any legal issues or questions that he, as the judge, would have to resolve. The judge was also a marine. To me there seemed to be a certain comradery between the judge and the prosecutor that went beyond both of them being officers in the Marine Corps. Knowing that from its beginning in 1798 until 1942, the United States Marine Corps excluded blacks from its ranks, this court-martial was beginning to take on an aura that would not bode well for my client. Those factors began to make me feel uneasy. During that chamber conference with the judge, I surmised that he knew the factual contours of this case and had already developed an opinion. Judges are to make rulings in a case based solely on the facts that are developed during the trial. From his demeanor during the rest of that chamber conference, any hope of this judge being impartial was unceremoniously put to rest.

Hoping against hope, I still believed, when confronted with the evidence in this case, the military judge would do what was right. That hope was quashed completely during *voir dire* (the preliminary examination of the witness). A military jury is made up of servicemembers, commissioned and noncommissioned officers. The judge appoints what is referred to as the President of the Board. In this case, the jury would consist of seven persons. I was allowed to ask questions of the prospective jurors. A white, male Navy Commissioned Officer from Indiana was called as a prospective juror. Understanding that this case had a significant racial tinge attached to it, I asked each prospective juror if they were against or had any problems with black men dating or having an intimate sexual relationship with a white woman. When that question was posed to the white commissioned male officer, he answered in the affirmative. I further pressed him, through questioning, for the foundation of his belief. **He replied that he was always taught that the races should remain separate**. At this point, I thought that surely this judge would disqualify the officer from service on the jury. When I made the motion for his disqualification, the judge asked this white officer if he could be fair. He said that he could. The judge denied my motion and allowed this officer to sit on the jury. He made this commissioned officer president of the board (the jury foreman). While I was emotionally stunned by the military judge's ruling, I concluded that, strategically, this was not the best point in the trial to reap maximum benefit from a display of my outrage. Further, an unbridled response to the judge's ruling would have conveyed to the prosecutor and the military judge that they were succeeding in trying to dishevel my game plan for trying this case. A jury of two commissioned officers, three noncommissioned officers, and two service members were impaneled. One of the servicemembers was a black seaman. There were no females on the jury. I believed, because I had to, that out of the seven members on the court-martial board, I perhaps could convince four that my client was not guilty.

I realize that there was a concerted effort between the military court judge, prosecutor, and certain members of the jury to convict this black sailor. His crime was that he had the audacity to have sex with a white woman.

As the trial began, the prosecutor called an expert to validate the findings from the rape kit. During cross-examination, I got the expert to admit that there was no hair from an African-American male found in the vaginal area or any other place on the alleged victim's body. I further grilled him on whether naval criminal investigators should have gathered evidence from the berth where the female shipmate was supposedly raped. The expert's response was that they should have. This line of questioning during cross-examination was aimed at the sloppiness or better yet, downright negligence of the investigators in their probe of the so-called rape. My thought was that if in fact they truly wanted to determine whether a rape occurred, they would have done a forensic analysis of the bed sheets or covering in the berthing area where the supposed sexual encounter occurred. The expert had to admit that although the evidence showed my client's semen in the vaginal cavity of the white shipmate, he could not say with any degree of medical certainty, how long it had been there or whether it was there because of a forcible encounter between my client and the white female shipmate. He did admit, as I facetiously grilled him, that my client was not Caucasian and the pubic hair that was found in the vaginal area of the alleged victim could not have been my client's. He admitted that the hair found on the victim was that of a Caucasian man. Only the chief investigator testified. His testimony was absolutely terrible. He and his team did not interview any of the other female berth mates of the alleged victim. The crux of his testimony was that my client admitted having sex with the white female shipmate. However,

Mr. Johnson never admitted that he had forcible sex with the white female shipmate on the day of the alleged rape.

The investigator was not able to provide any explanation as to why pubic hair of a black man was not found in the vaginal area of the alleged rape victim. He too admitted that there was no evidence, that the Navy had to refute the statement of the defendant that the sexual intercourse that occurred between the female Caucasian shipmate and the defendant did not happen off the base. Also, he could not dispute, in any fashion, that the sexual encounters of the defendant and the female shipmate were other than consensual.

When the investigator interviewed the female shipmate, there were no bruises or abrasions on her body.

As I gingerly treaded into this area, let it be clearly understood that I am thoroughly, without hesitation, against nonconsensual sexual encounters. That said, I was equally committed to preventing, as best I could, my client from becoming a display for a system that would punish consensual interracial intercourse. Finally, the prosecutor called the alleged victim to testify. She was dressed in her military uniform. Her hair was well manicured. But in a military court-martial, I didn't expect anything less. As she entered the courtroom, the jury turned their attention exclusively to the supposed victim. While answering questions from the prosecutor, she volunteered very little in terms of testimony. She was very uncomfortable. The prosecutor, as I did, realized that her testimony was ambivalent at best. He never asked her about having a consensual sexual relationship with the defendant away from the naval base. I viewed this as fertile ground to be plowed on cross-examination. She rambled through this allegation of my client entering the female berthing quarters and forcing her to have sex with him. In midstream of this critical testimony, she began to profusely shed tears. But these were not tears of outrage or hurt. All during this very tearful segment of her testimony, she was looking at me and my client. Her facial expressions revealed a notion of I am sorry for having to do this and for being forced to testify about our relationship. This crying was, although genuine, apologetic. My memory is faulty on this point, but I believe the trial judge took a recess so that the prosecutor could regain control over the victim. That move by the trial judge confirmed in my mind that he was going to do everything he could to convict this black sailor for having sex with his white female shipmate. But the crying did not stop. After a couple of questions by the prosecutor that the victim could not answer because of her emotional state, the prosecutor, a marine, had no further questions.

As I got up to cross-examine the victim, I vividly realized that there could not be scorch-earth questions asked. Instantaneously, I reminded myself of the comedian Richard Pryor. In one of his jokes, Mr. Pryor related an account of being married to a white woman whom he was divorcing. At the final hearing, to paraphrase Mr. Pryor, he said that the judge started crying with his wife as she was crying while testifying. In his comedic manner, Mr. Pryor reported that the judge said, "Mr. Pryor we want everything and if you have any dreams, we want those to." My cross-examination had to be gentle, but persuasive. It was clear to me, and I hoped to the military jury as well, that this supposed victim did not want to be in this proceeding and was being forced to testify against this black sailor. It was obvious to me that she had a romantic sexual relationship with this black sailor. The question for me was, *how could I convince a jury of military men that this sexual liaison was consensual and did not occur on the ship?* And even if I could, would it matter to this jury? Up to that point in the trial, I could sense a certain pressure that was being imposed upon the jury members by the command structure for a guilty verdict. I had no evidence that would prove she was being forced by the command structure to testify that my client raped her.

Although the evidence presented to that point in the trial would have probably resulted in a dismissal of these charges in civilian court, I had no faith that the same would be true in this court-martial before this Judge. The alleged victim never, with any definitiveness, said that my client raped her. Her testimony regarding him entering into the female berthing area was sketchy at best. She admitted not reporting this supposed rape to anyone until she was confronted by her master chief. The master chief was a white male of Southern origin. She did, in a roundabout way, testify that she was encouraged to report an alleged rape by the master chief. I pressed her, through precise questions, on the finding from the rape Vitullo kit about the pubic hair of a white male found in her vaginal area. The supposed victim admitted to having more than one sexual partner.

During cross-examination, she indicated that there was another man who was Caucasian. He was also a shipmate. This should not be construed to disparage or in any way do damage to a legitimate rape victim. I was convinced that this female was not a victim of rape. If anything, she was a victim of being pressured by the command structure on her ship to maintain the good order by keeping a black male sailor in his place. By extension the treatment of this black male sailor would send a very definite message to other black males on the ship that having a sexual liaison with a white female crewmember would be met with severe punishment. She could not explain how, given the closeness of the berthing quarters, no one else saw my client enter the area where she slept. When I asked her whether the alleged rape in the berthing quarters was forcible, she began to sob uncontrollably. To me that would have been enough for a dismissal of this case by the trial judge. But this crewcut Marine military court judge in his mid-fifties was having none of that. He allowed the case to go to the military jury for them to make a decision.

Given the fact that he had made the commission officer from Indiana, who clearly expressed a dislike for black-white relationships, the jury's foreman, I knew that a guilty verdict was forthcoming. It was at that point that I unleashed a verbal barrage at this racist military judge that was totally unrestrained. While some, who read these words, may think that what I perceived to be eloquent outlay of the law and the facts of this case was untimely, my conclusion was that I had nothing to lose and everything to gain. My words were so profound to the ears of this skinhead marine, he threatened to jail me. I knew that was a veiled threat, at best, because not being a member of the military, he had no jurisdiction to levy any fines or other consequences against me. And without any verbal restraints, I let him know that.

In the military, the commanding officer can set aside or lessen any punishment rendered in a court-martial. My strategy was to hopefully get the commanding officer of the naval base to set aside or exonerate my client. That did not happen. This was a tragedy of monumental proportions. As I expected, the military jury came back, after a brief deliberation, with a guilty verdict. This black sailor was guilty of having consensual sex with a white woman. Nothing adverse happened to the shipmate who was allegedly raped. My client was sentenced time in prison and given a dishonorable discharge. To this day, I am still haunted by the outcome from this kangaroo court.

CHAPTER 20

Public Defender–Client Arrested for Possession While He Was a Passenger in a Car Driven by a White Male

Since its inception, the court system in South Carolina has never been fair and equitable to people of color. Black defendants in the criminal courts of South Carolina are routinely sentenced and fined more harshly than similarly situated white persons.

The deep-seated historical disproportionate sentencing of black defendants, as opposed to their white counterparts, is still so very prevalent in the American judicial system. It matters not whether the black defendants are in federal or state court. In 2009, a federal judge by the name of T. S. Ellis, III., sentenced a black congressman, William Jefferson of Louisiana, to thirteen years in prison for using his office as a criminal enterprise to enrich himself. Prior to that time, no white member of Congress had ever been sentenced to jail for such a long time on similar charges. Up to that point, the longest prison sentence ever received by a member of Congress was eight years. His name was Randy Cunningham. Of course, he was white.

By contrast, the same Federal Judge, T. S. Ellis, III., sentenced Paul Manafort to forty-seven months in prison for criminal conduct much more egregious than that of former congressman William Jefferson. Even when Manafort was sentenced a second time by another federal judge for additional crimes, his cumulative sentence amounted to a mere seven and one-half years. The crimes Jefferson committed, were in no way as flagrant as those committed by Manafort. That judge, according to the *New York Times*, stated in the sentencing hearing that, *"Manafort had used his many talents as a strategist to evade taxes, deceive banks, subvert lobbying laws and obstruct justice – all so he could sustain an "ostentatiously opulent" lifestyle with "more houses than a family can enjoy, more suits than one man can wear."* No such observations are found in the transcript of the sentencing hearing for the black congressman William Jefferson. Yet, he was sentenced to thirteen years while Manafort got a combined sentence of seven and one-half years from two different federal judges.

In 1963, a unanimous United States Supreme Court decided in the case *of Gideon v. Wainwright,* that every defendant in a criminal proceeding has a constitutional right to an attorney to represent their interests. In part, the court opinion reads, *"reason and reflection require us to recognize that in our adversary system of criminal justice, any person haled into court, who is too poor to hire a lawyer, cannot be assured a fair trial unless counsel is provided for him."* Justice Black, who wrote the opinion for the court, also stated that, *"the "noble ideal" of "fair trials before impartial tribunals in which every defendant stands equal before the law… cannot be realized if the poor man charged with crime has to face his accusers without a lawyer to assist him."*

Because of this decision, most states established the public defender system. In theory then, every defendant charged with a crime and was too poor to afford a lawyer would be provided one by the state. In practice, for most defendants, this public defender's office is treacherous at best. State legislatures have repeatedly underfunded public defender's offices. In 2016, Barry Pollack, President of the National Association of Criminal Defense Lawyers said, *"The promise of competent counsel with sufficient time and resources to devote to a defendant's case has never been truly fulfilled... Underfunding of public defenders and public defense in this country has been a chronic problem really sense the inception of the Gideon v. Wainwright decision..."* According to an article written by Alan Greenblatt, public defender lawyers have felony caseloads of five to six times more than what is recommended by the American Bar Association. Thus, the lack of funding and exorbitant caseloads create a recipe for disaster for poor defendants. Perhaps it was stated best by Walter Sanchez, an attorney from Lake Charles, Louisiana, in an article in *The Advocate Newspaper.* Mr. Sanchez said, *"Candidly, the current system fails its responsibility to deliver quality services. As a result of that, individual defendants who are represented by public defenders across the state are at risk of ineffective assistance of counsel."*

Most black defendants in criminal court do not have the financial resources to hire competent attorneys to protect their interests. However, while it is presented to the defendant that the representation is free, it is not. In order for a defendant to be screened by the Public Defender's office so that a determination can be made as to whether or not that defendant is entitled to their services, there is a cost. The Public Defender's Office is not designed for the purpose of trying cases on a regular basis in the criminal justice system. They have an ongoing and close relationship with the Prosecutor's Office and in some instances personnel from both offices interchange positions.

After an initial interview with the defendants they represent, most public defenders, because of the work overload, do not meet with their clients until very close to or the day of trial. This arrangement is troublesome for the defendant. Most of the time, in this situation, the defendant is confronted with a plea deal from the prosecutor's office. Prior to the deal being offered, there has been very little, if any, substantive discussion between the public defender and the defendant. The defendant, whom it seems is always poor and black, is pressured into a guilty plea because of the fear that going to trial would result in a much longer period of incarceration if found guilty.

I have witnessed this scenario more times than I care to remember. On one occasion, I was retained by the family members of a defendant who was represented by a public defender. That defendant, who was black, was a passenger in a car driven by a white male. There was another passenger who was white. The driver was giving my client a ride home from a party. Two North Charleston, South Carolina, police officers stopped the car. My client was in the back seat literally intoxicated lying face up. The two white police officers decided to arrest the passenger, my client. Both the white driver and the other passenger were allowed to go about their business.

On the police report they wrote that the client gave them permission to search his body and low and behold, they found a quantity of marijuana and cocaine. The first thing that made my spine chill was how in God's name could these two officers represent to a court that a black man, who was totally inebriated, have the consciousness to give them consent to search anything, much less his body, for contrabands. The report, written by the two police officers, succinctly stated that my client was so drunk that he had to be put in a special detox unit upon being incarcerated in the Charleston County

Jail. This client was particularly vulnerable to the extent that he had two prior convictions. A plea or guilty verdict on the charges of possession of cocaine and marijuana would have exposed him to approximately fifteen years in prison because of the enhancement statute. Generally, the enhancement statute allows a court to significantly increase the penalty to be imposed on the defendant if the offense which he has pled guilty to or found guilty of is a third offense.

After getting my client's files from the public defender's office, there was no evidence that a preliminary hearing was requested. I cannot imagine given what was on the police report, why this notion of the defendant being able to give permission to the arresting officers to search his personage was not challenged by the lawyer from the public defender's office. The ethnicity and gender of the public defender was Caucasian and female. My client was a black male. I found nothing in the documents that my client retrieved from the public defender's office that indicated a zealous representation of this client. After reviewing those documents, my conclusion was that a more than credible argument could have be made that this client was not being represented by a lawyer. Or maybe, because he was black and had two previous convictions, it would not have been a good use of time trying to defend him. Many defendants' liberties are sacrificed because of this lack of competent legal representation.

I was never more committed to make sure that this client was not sentenced to prison for fifteen years because two Caucasian cops from the city of North Charleston decided that they were going to pad their records of convictions for felonies against another African-American. The public defender, who was representing this client before the family retained my services, was prepared to allow him to plead guilty and receive twelve and one-half years under the enhancement statute.

Of course, I filed the various constitutional motions, including one to suppress to prevent this tragedy from occurring. The prosecutor read the same police report that I did. Given what was reflected in the report, I thoroughly believed this was a case which the prosecutor would dismiss because the officers could not have gained consent from my client to search him. It was logical then to believe and assume the right thing would be done by the prosecutorial authorities. My beliefs were quickly dispelled during my first telephonic conversation with this prosecutor. First he was ambivalent about my position regarding my client being too drunk to give the police the authority to search him. About three weeks later, we had a second telephone conversation about this critical fact. As I remember, I asked him how could my client give permission to the police officer to search him if he was drunk? I reminded him that one of the arresting officers said in his report that my client was incapacitated to the point of being unable to respond to any of the officers' commands. His responses danced around providing any meaningful answer. In further pressing him on this issue, he indicated that he would think about my position and we would talk later. In the ensuing conversations with the prosecutor, of which there were three, he never agreed to dismiss the case.

On November 20, 2000, I was notified by the prosecutor's office at about 2:30 p.m. that the case would be called at trial the next day at 10:00 a.m. I arrived to the courtroom around 8:30 a.m. with the intent to have one last conference with the prosecutor. Our conversations became a little heated. The reason for this procrastination about dismissing the case finally revealed itself. He informed me that he could not make me a better offer than he made to the public defender. To me, for this young man to go to jail for twelve and a half years would have been a travesty. The combative nature of my spirit rose to the surface. Almost extemporaneously to this young and obviously inexperienced prosecutor I said that, "When we get in the courtroom to argue this motion for suppression, I'm going to open up a can of whip ass on you." In criminal cases constitutional motions are usually heard by the trial judge before the actual trial of the case begins. If the defendant prevails on the motion, normally the case is over. The constitutional motion filed in this case was to suppress any evidence the police officers could present at trial because the search and/or arrest of my client was illegal. Thus, the marijuana and cocaine that these officers allegedly found in my client's pants pockets could not be introduced as evidence by the prosecutor in the trial of this case.

In order to properly defend a client, especially in a criminal case, the lawyer must do the necessary investigations. I was able to locate the white passenger who was in the car when my client was arrested by these two North Charleston police officers. During my interview with him, he said he was willing to testify that he did not hear the police officers ask my client any questions, much less could they search him. Further, he told me that my client was sloppy drunk lying face up on the rear seat.

During that hearing, the trial judge listened to the testimony from the two police officers. At the suppression hearing, under cross-examination, one of the police officers admitted that my client could not and did not follow any of the commands that they gave to him while he was in the back seat of the car driven by the Caucasian male. They further admitted, under cross-examination, that my client stayed in the detox unit for a period of more than eight hours after being arrested. When asked how could my client give consent if he could not respond to the commands that they presented to him at the initial stop, one of the officers stated, "He could not." After giving that answer, and by the look on the officer's face, he realized that he had been caught in a lie in open court when he stated that the client gave him consent to search his personage. Coupled with the testimony from the white passenger about the conduct of both officers towards this defendant, the trial judge granted my motion to suppress any introduction into evidence of the marijuana and cocaine in the prosecution of this case. That was enough for the trial judge to dismiss this case on constitutional grounds. No one on behalf of the defendant had ever contacted or interviewed this white passenger. Had my client pled guilty, as was suggested by the public defender, he would have been sentenced to a minimum of ten years in prison. This kind of transaction is very commonplace, especially with the poor and black defendants. It permeates the American criminal justice system.

CHAPTER 21

The Federal Court System

F or the purposes of this chapter, a very brief verbal schematic diagram of the federal judiciary is necessary. The very first level of this system is the United States District Court. Going up the totem pole, the next court is the Circuit Courts of Appeals, and at the very top sits the United States Supreme Court. The District Court is the workhorse of the federal judiciary. Except in very few instances, most Americans' first encounter with the federal courts begin in the District Court. There are some instances where cases filed by aggrieved parties are assigned to a United States Magistrate. These are individuals, usually with a legal background, who conduct preliminary matters relating to a case on behalf of the United States District Court judge to which the case has been assigned. The federal judiciary is, by no stretch of the imagination, immune from the institutionalized racism that pervades this country.

One of the most perverse and vicious attacks ever levied upon me in open court was authored by a United States magistrate. I had an action pending in the federal court. There was a hearing scheduled on a substantive issue before this United States magistrate. Initially, I received notice from the court that the hearing was scheduled at 10:00 a.m. Around 9:00 a.m. on the morning of the hearing, my office received a call from the magistrate judge's clerk indicating that the hearing had been postponed until 2:00 p.m. I arrived at the courthouse around 1:30 p.m. to make sure that I was on time for the hearing. I'd never appeared before this federal magistrate. As I walked into the courtroom, there were about twenty-five lawyers seated and none had the hue of my epidermis. The magistrate was conducting another hearing and in the middle of that hearing, without pause, he informed me that I was late and in contempt of court for not appearing at 10:00 a.m. I was further told that I was going to be fined by the court the sum of $200. Instantaneously, I responded that while it was within his preview to hold me in contempt, I had a right to have my day in court and I went to my seat to wait to be heard on the motion for which I was appearing. I didn't know the *"son of a bitch,"* but I did know that he was not going to use me as a mechanism to display his outright racism. It was clear that his motive was to embarrass me and perhaps make himself look bigger in front of all of the Caucasian lawyers. After I informed him that I wanted to be heard on being held in contempt of court, his face turned red. My mind raced to a contentious posture premised upon the knowledge that there was verbal communication from his clerk memorialized on my office's message pad that the hearing on the motion had been rescheduled to 2:00 p.m. I decided that there was no set of circumstances under which I would acquiesce to allow this bastard to hold me in contempt. That was not happening, not on that day. As I sat waiting for this judge to hear my motion, I knew that he was going to try to make my appearance as excruciatingly painful as possible. My thoughts reverted back to the admonition of my law school Professor Roberson King. He taught me that you must be twice as good and more prepared than your adversary in the courtroom because you will, on many occasions, have to educate the person donning the robe. I had read all of the case laws that I needed and was prepared. A peaceful calm occupied my mind. Nothing he was going to say or do would shake my resolve. And if he ruled against me, I was going to appeal and get his ruling reversed.

About forty-five minutes later, the motion for which I was appearing was heard. A number of the white lawyers were still in the courtroom. After I started and during my oral argument on the motion, the magistrate repeatedly interrupted me with, what I thought were, nonsensical questions because they had no bearing on the substance of the motion. I was on top of my game and determined not to be derailed. The hearing went on for about thirty minutes. The attorney opposing the motion was never interrupted during his argument nor asked any questions. After opposing counsel finished with his comments, the judge asked me if I had anything further. I replied, "No except that I needed a day certain to be heard on the contempt of court declaration." He then informed us that he would take the motion for which I was allegedly late, under advisement. That meant he would not be ruling on the motion from the bench on that day. As it turned out, in the interim the case was settled and the motion became moot.

About five days later, the magistrate's clerk called my office to inform me that there would be no need for a hearing on the contempt matter because the magistrate had reversed himself. After that hearing, I hoped that I never had an occasion to appear before this United States magistrate again. However, that was not to be.

Nepotism was a lifestyle at the Charleston Naval Shipyard. More than seventy-five percent of the people who worked there were related to each other. Upon graduating from high school, a white person that secured a job at the shipyard could expect to work there, except in rare cases, until retirement. Indeed, for them it was an easy life.

In an employment discrimination case, I represented a black woman by the name of Courtney Smith. Ms. Smith was incredibly smart and gifted as an accountant. She also taught as an adjunct professor at one of the local colleges. Ms. Smith worked for a division of the Department of Defense. That agency is called the Defense Finance and Accounting Services (DFAS). Ms. Smith was a few hours short of securing her doctoral degree in an accounting-related field. When she started working for DFAS, her third line supervisor was a white woman, Samantha Harris, that had, at best, a high school diploma. Ms. Harris was absorbed by that agency after the closure of the Charleston Naval Base. When the Charleston shipyard closed in the late 1990s, many of the employees were given options to be placed at other locations or agencies. One vehicle employed by the Federal Government to facilitate this goal was the Priority Placement Program. If an employee was minimally qualified to be offered a job with another agency, they would be placed with that agency. The operative words here are minimally qualified. A number of naval shipyard employees were placed in management jobs at other agencies for which they were imminently not qualified. More than seventy-five percent of the time that practice benefited Caucasian employees. Ms. Smith's first and second-line supervisors were black. The director of the site where Ms. Smith worked was a Caucasian male. He would be considered her fifth line supervisor. Ms. Smith applied, repeatedly, for promotions and supervisory positions. She always made the best qualified list but was never promoted based on subjective criteria of an all-white selection panel.

After repeatedly not being promoted, she approached and complained to the site Equal Employment Opportunity

Commission director. Ms. Smith and I later learned the site director was incensed about Ms. Smith complaining of race discrimination. The site director then decided to placate her. They sent her to a management program in Orlando, Florida. As was later revealed, Ms. Smith's initial complaint of discriminatory treatment set in motion a series of retaliatory actions against her by all in her supervisory chain, including Samantha Harris. Ms. Harris was the deputy director of civilian pay at the Defense Finance and Accounting Services (DFAS). Except for the color of her skin, I was never presented with a reason that justified her becoming the Deputy Director without formal education beyond high school. In fact, Ms. Harris was assumedly trying to get a college degree, and she was a student in a class at the local college taught by Ms. Smith.

When Ms. Smith returned to the Charleston site, her immediate supervisor was an African-American female. She was harassed daily. We later discovered through documents that had to be produced by DFAS after we filed the lawsuit, that there was an attorney working for the agency located in Cleveland, Ohio who was giving daily directions to Ms. Smith's first and second-line supervisors as to what to do to her. In fact I remember an email from one of the DFAS attorneys in Cleveland that said, *"what can we do today to make Ms. Smith more miserable?"*

Ms. Smith applied for various promotions and was selected for a position in Illinois. She was given a date to report to her new position. A couple days before she was to leave for Illinois, she received an email from the selecting official telling her that her application should not have been considered and that she was not the person that should have been selected. There was an email from her fifth line supervisor, the Caucasian male, to the Illinois selecting official that Ms. Smith was an EEOC troublemaker and should not be a part of the organization. During the deposition of the fifth line supervisor, he stated that personnel decisions never come on his radar screen. He also stated, under oath, that he had no knowledge as to why the position offered to Ms. Smith in Illinois was withdrawn. When I presented the email he had written to the selecting official in Illinois, all were stunned. He began to stutter, perspire, and look dumbfounded. The attorney representing DFAS was ready to give up.

Ms. Smith needed to take some time off because of personal matters. She filed all the necessary documents to the letter and followed all procedures to secure the leave. After returning from leave, she was given notice by Samantha Harris that she would be suspended for being AWOL. Mind you, this was just one of many retaliatory events that the agency instigated against my client. Every time there was discriminatory conduct or a retaliatory event toward Ms. Smith, I would file a complaint with the EEOC.

A complaint with the EEOC would trigger a process by which the person being discriminated against could ask for a hearing before an administrative law judge. Before the hearing was held the person complaining of discrimination was allowed to do limited discovery in prosecuting their case before the EEOC. The taking of depositions was also allowed. My strategy was to always forward Requests for Production and Interrogatories to the agency. After receiving responses, I would take the depositions of the agency's key witnesses. If and when the case was filed in the United States District Court, a much broader discovery process was allowed. While this method was time-consuming and, in some instances duplicitous, it was necessary in order to prevail. In depositions, once the agency's witnesses testified, they would be very hard-pressed to change the initial testimony given in the first deposition. I always relish getting the emails that had to be produced in the proceeding filed in the United States District Court. One or more of those emails invariably would contain a proverbial smoking gun.

A set of facts are developed for these kinds of cases. This case was slightly unique. Based on the emails that the agency was required to give us after we filed a lawsuit, it became clear to me that DFAS had used one of the oldest, yet effective, tactics in trying to get rid of Ms. Smith because she complained of race discrimination. Both of her black supervisors were promised promotions if they helped the agency fire Ms. Smith. The divide and conquer strategy (The Crab Syndrome) that had been (and is still being) used by the majority population when it comes to black people. Ms. Smith's case was ultimately settled. Neither her nor I were unhappy with the amount of the settlement.

It was clients like Ms. Smith who had the desire to fight for what is right, but not the inclination to hate those who perpetrated the wrong that furthered my desire to fight and win these battles. These are battles that must be fought and won, and as fate would have it, the United States magistrate that did his best to embarrass me in front of all of the white lawyers played a pivotal role in encouraging the government to conclude Ms. Smith's case. And for that, I now thank him.

CHAPTER 22

The Crab Syndrome

On the banks of the James River in 1712, a speech was purportedly given by a slave owner named William Lynch. Supposedly, Lynch said the following words:

"Gentlemen, I greet you here on the bank of the James River in the year of our Lord one thousand seven hundred and twelve. First, I shall thank you, the gentlemen of the Colony of Virginia, for bringing me here. I am here to help you solve some of your problems with slaves. Your invitation reached me on my modest plantation in the West Indies where I have experimented with some of the newest and still the oldest methods for control of slaves. Ancient Rome would envy us if my program is implemented. As our boat sailed south on the James River, named for our illustrious King, whose version of the Bible we cherish, I saw enough to know that your problem is not unique. While Rome used cords of wood as crosses for standing human bodies along its old highways in great numbers you are here using the tree and the rope on occasion.

I caught a whiff of a dead slave hanging from a tree a couple of miles back. You are not only losing valuable stock by hangings, you are having uprisings, slaves are running away, your crops are sometimes less in the fields too long for maximum profit, you can suffer occasional fires, your animals are killed. Gentlemen, you know what your problems are; I do not need to elaborate. I am not here to enumerate your problems, I am here to introduce you to a method of solving them. In my bag here, I have a fool proof method for controlling your Black slaves. I guarantee everyone of you that if installed correctly it will control the slaves for at least 300 years. My method is simple. Any member of your family or your overseer can use it.

I have outlined a number of differences among the slaves; and I have taken these differences and make them bigger. I use fear, distrust, and envy for control purposes. These methods have worked on my modest plantation in the West Indies and it will work throughout the South. Take this simple little list of differences and think about them. On top of my list is "Age", the second is "Color" or shade, there is intelligence, size, sex, size of plantations, status on the plantation, attitude of owners, whether the slaves live in the valley, on the hill, East, West, North, South, have fine hair or coarse hair, or is tall or short. Now that you have a list of differences, I shall give you an outline of action-but before that I shall assure you that distrust is stronger than adulation; respect or admiration.

The Black slave after receiving this indoctrination shall carry on and will become self re-fueling and self-generating for hundreds of years, maybe thousands.

Don't forget you must pitch the old Black vs. the young Black male, and the young Black male against the old Black male. You must use the dark skin slave vs. the light skin slaves and the light skin slaves vs. the dark skin slaves. You must use the female vs. the male, and the male vs. the female. You must also have your White servants and overseers distrust all Blacks, but it is necessary that your slaves trust and depend on us. They must love, respect, and trust only us.

Gentlemen, these Kits are your Keys to control. Use them. Have your wives and children use them, never miss opportunity. If used intensely for one year, the slaves themselves will remain perpetually distrustful."

There are significant questions about the authenticity of this speech. It has been concluded by a number of historians to be a hoax. My purpose here is not to shed light on the genuineness or legitimacy of the speech of William Lynch. It is mentioned as a backdrop from which, in large measures, served as a blueprint for over 350 years of America's treatment of African-Americans. It is of no consequence to me that William Lynch may not have spoken those words. But who among us can, with truthfulness, argue against the fact that the concepts in the alleged speech of Mr. Lynch do not constitute a verbal portrait of America and its black citizens?

Unfortunately, for us as black people, some of those constructs are still employed by some of the majority population. One of the most damnable phenomena that has been used by institutions in perpetuating institutionalized racism is getting one minority to do damage to another of the same race. The minority that administers the damage is promised rewards for their efforts. Here's how it works. A supervisory employee, usually a white person, solicits, with a promise of promotion or other rewards, a black employee to assist in doing harm to another black employee. This was a particularly troubling obstacle to overcome in an employment discrimination case. Courts are usually loath to believe that a black employee will discriminate against another black employee because of his or her race. I have been confronted with this situation on numerous occasions.

I represented a very bright African-American nurse who was smarter than her nurse executive. The nurse executive was a white female. She felt threatened by the African-American nurse because that nurse was more pedigreed than her supervisor, the white nurse executive. Unfortunately for my client, she had been employed at the federal agency for only about a year and a half. My client was still in the probationary period. The white, female nurse executive followed none of the protocols in evaluating the performance of my client during her brief tenure at the federal agency. My client had innovative, as well as cost-saving programs that she developed for the purpose of saving the federal agency money and making it more efficient in rendering services to veterans. Those programs were going to be presented at national seminars held by the federal agency. The white nurse executive became resentful that this black nurse was receiving invitations from national organizations to present her programs. The white nurse executive decided to convene a board to determine whether or not my client was fit for the position. Most federal agencies have a probationary period for new hires. During that period, which is usually one to two years, an employee can be terminated pretty much without cause. However, an employee cannot be terminated during that probationary period because of their race, sex, or national origin. Realizing that she had no reason to terminate my client, other than the fact that my client was black, the nurse executive and others above her in leadership at the federal agency, put on the board a black female, a black male, and one white male. The hearing before the board was really perfunctory. The decision to terminate my client had already been made. During the hearing, I had to take a bathroom break. I could not find the bathroom. The black male nurse manager on the board came out of the room and directed me to the bathroom. I asked him why my client was being tried by this board on an issue that was completely minute. He explained to me that he was sorry, but the decision to remove my client from the agency had already been made. His purpose there was cursory at best. During the hearing, the black female nurse manager was particularly accusatory in regards to this alleged non-consequential protocol that my client was accused of not following. My client and I later discovered, as if we didn't already know, the black male nurse was given a job that constituted a promotion in another federal agency office in the State of Maryland. The black female nurse manager was stationed at one of the satellite offices of the main federal agency and wanted to be promoted to a position in the Central office. Both of those black nurse managers were rewarded for their efforts in terminating my client from the federal agency. True or not, William Lynch's speech rang true for my client. Her life was totally disrupted. That would not have been accomplished without the two black nurse managers being used by the federal agency's leadership to accomplish that end.

One of my clients filed a charge of race discrimination against her supervisor. Practically speaking, especially with regards to federal agencies, there is little protection for the person that initiates such a charge. Once a charge is officially made by way of some writing to an outside agency for investigation purposes, an unwritten process with deadly precision begins to operate. The name of the black person making the allegation of race discrimination against his or her white supervisor spreads throughout. All efforts, almost in a maniacal way, are made to retaliate against all black persons making the charge of discrimination. While I have no personal knowledge of meetings being held for the purpose of constructing a plan to harass the race discrimination complainant, it never fails that the life of that individual becomes hell at work. The purpose of this conduct by management or leadership is to penalize the complainant in such a manner, so as to prevent others from choosing that path. The leadership mindset is that you are not to complain and should in fact enjoy being kicked in your ass because of your race. Perhaps this notion of supremacy is best described by an exchange between one of my clients and her white supervisor. The supervisor said, *"be thankful that you have a job."* If the complainant continues to go forth with the charge of race discrimination, more often than not, they are terminated. Sometimes that result occurs even if the complainant has an attorney to represent their interests in the discrimination case. It does not matter what their performance evaluation was prior to the charge of discrimination being filed. In most cases, all of a sudden, a good employee with excellent evaluations becomes one with less than satisfactory performance evaluations.

CHAPTER 23

The Sisterhood

The practice of law, at least to me, was not the proper vehicle by which something transformative could be done to alleviate the injustices against people of color in the American judicial system. There were many times that I felt so limited in trying to correct the systemic racism. I experienced relentless struggles with the inability through one case to address a host of issues based on race discrimination. Clients would recant facts of vicious institutional-wide race discrimination. Most of them wanted to and thought they could use their case to make right all of the racial problems at their place of employment. Ironically, I had to bridle those expectations and desires so that I could be successful in representing that client. My constant refrain was we could not use the facts of this case to correct all the wrongs in the world. I explained, "I am here to represent you and to get you the best results that I can. Bringing about successful results in your case, does not allow me to rectify all of the racially-based wrongs at your job." I would sympathize with the client's desire, but knew that my effort had to be constricted to a successful monetary result for that client. For many years I tried to come up with the method by which the success I was having in employment discrimination cases could be more meaningful than just getting a handsome financial conclusion for that one client.

Some would say that a class action lawsuit is always available to individuals who believe that the class to which they belong is being treated improperly because of their race. For an attorney who practices law by himself, the class action vehicle is impracticable. Class action cases are very difficult to manage, over burdensome with work, and can very easily consume the sole practitioner like me. Class action lawsuits can go on for a decade or more. For a lawyer practicing alone, that would be financially catastrophic. I convinced myself that I had to be satisfied with the single case successes. While my cases were not as game-changing, I took refuge in the fact that I corrected the wrongs committed against each client, respectively. The notoriety of being successful in one case at a time is priceless. For clients would spread the good news of being excellently represented through word-of-mouth. That was how I built my law practice.

The opportunity to try to make a fundamental dent into institutionalized racism presented itself on more than one occasion. The first was when I represented three black female principal and assistant principals. **Because of their single-minded desire to rebel against the racist policies and practices of the Charleston County School Board, I ultimately represented them in their revolt.** The first time they came to me about representation, I referred them to a Caucasian attorney. That attorney had some previous success against the School Board. After meeting with that attorney, the three black administrators told me that the white attorney told them they didn't have a case. Hell, I knew that analysis was not true. Upon reflection, I was willing to convince myself I was not up to representing these three black female educators. In that initial conference, my thoughts wondered. If I said yes to their request for representation, that would mean a significant disruption of my then well-established daily routine. At that point, I fancied myself as being semi-retired (and often lived the retired lifestyle). My days were pretty much mine to do as I pleased. I would not be able to play golf on a regular basis. Stresses would develop causing loss of sleep, among other things. I would be consumed in preparing to be successful in the representation of these black educators.

At the second meeting, I still was not convinced that this was an enterprise I should undertake. One of my children got wind of my hesitancy and told me that they were surprised about me not wanting to represent these administrators. My daughter further scolded me with my own words to her. She said, "You always taught me to stand up for right. Why are you not living up to those words?" After hearing those words, frankly, I was ashamed of myself. They had a good case and no one to represent them. That changed immediately. I realized this was going to be a titanic battle against the school district, but having been shamed by my child, I reasoned *let the war begin.*

These women had terminal degrees and were overwhelmingly qualified to be principals and assistant principals. They complained, vehemently, against the many and varied discriminatory efforts by the school district against black students and staff. The white school district leaders did not approve of these black female administrators complaining about race discrimination in the Charleston County School District. Their complaints were very grounded in reality.

A white teacher, with impunity, told a class of African-American students that when Barack Obama's term as president is over, they were going to be shipped back to Africa.

After a public outcry by black parents and students, that teacher was allowed to resign from that school. The very next school year, the teacher was hired at a predominantly white school in the district. White teachers would refer to black students as criminals, thugs, and drug dealers. Whenever a black administrator would complain about what he or she perceived as discriminatory conduct by white teachers, the district's leadership would engage in sinful endeavors to exact a punishment against the black administrator.

Black administrators were placed in very difficult and challenging schools by the school board or superintendent. In most instances, these administrators turned failing schools into excellent learning environments. In one instance, a team of black administrators was given the daunting task of turning around a virtually all-black school that had been failing for a period in excess of ten years. Within a period of less than three years, that school was thriving and very successful, according to the State Board of Education measuring tool. The local school board, through one of its superintendents, decided that this team, albeit successful in the mission that they were given, needed to be dismantled.

That was baffling, but not so much because later it became clear during the litigation, that the district school board wanted to close the ninety-eight percent black school for the purpose of accommodating the changing racial demographics of that community. Efforts in that thrust had been ongoing for quite some time. White parents did not want their children attending a school which was predominantly black although they lived in the attendance zone of the school. I was told by one white parent that they were tired of sending their children out of the attendance zone to predominantly white schools in the school district. The School Board, through its

Caucasian senior leadership, was doing their bidding. Truth be told, when these black administrators were assigned to the school, they were not expected to succeed in turning the school around. When they did in fact succeed, the plan to close the school that had been put in place, had to, yet again, be postponed.

What the school board did, through its superintendent, to perpetuate its projected closing of the dominantly black school, was to strip it of programs that would make the school very viable. For example, the school board decided that a nursing program that was prospering at the black school needed to be transferred to a predominantly white school. That kind of conduct designed to make the school less attractive would cause the student population to become smaller, resulting in a closure of the school.

I refer to these three black female administrators as the sisterhood. In order to bring about the desired results on behalf of these three black administrators, Ms. Adams, Ms. James, and Ms. Johnson, I embarked upon the strategy of bringing three separate lawsuits in the federal court against the school district. When a civil lawsuit is filed in the federal courts, the parties are allowed to engage in a wide variety of discovery or evidence gathering. Generally, there are two types of discovery that are allowed in the federal courts. There are written questions, commonly call interrogatories, and requests for production of relevant documents. In taking on an institution such as the school board, I needed to create the largest platform available to make the school district answer as many questions as I could, legally, and produce as many documents under the Federal rule regarding discovery. With three plaintiffs, I figured I would be able to secure all of the records from the school board that I would need to bring about a successful resolution of the litigation for my clients. The facts and situations of each of these plaintiffs' cases overlapped and were intertwined. Therefore, any record that I requested or question I asked would apply to all of my clients' cases. Also, I could depose any person the school board listed as a witness, on three separate occasions, correcting any mistake or covering any area that I did not touch upon in the previous deposition.

This was the most labor-intensive route to secure from the school district the evidence that my clients would need to be successful. It was, by no means, the easiest method. But then again, it has never been an easy path for black plaintiffs to have their rights vindicated in the American judicial system. Filing three separate lawsuits did not come without its traps. First, the cost in these cases were going to be somewhat expensive. The other gamble was that it would be extremely grueling to try these cases separately. Also, when we went to mediation, which is mandatory in the federal courts, there was going to be a very focused effort by the defendants to divide the plaintiffs by offering more money to one or two as opposed to the other. Every time we met, there was a reiteration of this fact, for I knew that was going to occur. We met quite often at my house on the back porch to discuss deposition testimony, interrogatories, and responses by the defendants to our interrogatories or request for production. Up to that point, I had never invited a client to my house to discuss their case. I felt such a kinship and such closeness to these educational giants. All reservations I harbored before regarding letting a client know where I lived went out of the window. Separate and apart from the facts of the case, I was so impressed with the sacrifices they made on a daily basis in their pursuit to educate all students, especially black children. We usually met on Saturday afternoons and I would prepare my fried whiting fish and salad.

The lawsuits named the school board as the defendant. That meant every member of the school board was a defendant and could be made to appear at a deposition so that their testimony could be taken under oath regarding the allegations of race discrimination in the school district. I knew that there were two black members of the school board who would have told the truth about race discrimination against black administrators, children, and teachers in the school district. Further, the school superintendent was quoted in the local newspaper admitting the Charleston School District had engaged in benign racism in regards to black children.

Over the course of the first four months after the litigation was filed, I forwarded to the defendants' attorney, a plethora of questions and documents to be produced regarding my clients' allegations of racism, racially motivated treatment, and the school district's failure to promote black administrators to the positions of principals, assistant principals, and associate superintendents. The defendants' attorney engaged in many delaying tactics in his efforts not to answer the interrogatories or produce the documents that were requested. The court would have none of it. We finally got to the point in the cases where the depositions of some of the defendants' witnesses were taken. For them, the defendants, those witnesses were disastrous. While none of them admitted that any of the actions toward the plaintiffs were racially motivated, they were hard-pressed to explain why they treated the plaintiffs so differently from their white counterparts who were similarly situated. None of them could provide a modicum of a credible explanation about the disproportionate disciplining and expulsion rate of black students as compared to white students.

The school system creates an extremely harsh disciplinary culture for non-white students. In the county where

I practice, for example, in the year 2016, approximately 8,200 students were suspended or expelled by the Charleston County School District. Of that number, in excess of 6,700 of those students were non-white. When confronted with the statistic in a lawsuit against the Charleston County School District, the proverbial answer was that our expulsion rate reflects a national problem and is not peculiar to us. That is not a response that should make anyone comfortable. Indeed, the school system in this county creates a school to prison pipeline.

The majority culture on the school board created a program, purportedly, to rectify this problem. The design of that program was fatally flawed, but constituted an appeasement for some of the citizens. Essentially, children who were expelled, were made to go to a designated school in the district for the purpose of continuing their learning. Those children, more than seventy-three percent black, had to find their own transportation to and from the designated school. After arriving, they were supposed to keep up with the classwork in the regular school by way of computers. There was rarely, if ever, a teacher to assist the students with their off-site educational pursuits. None of the other privileges associated with regular school, such as, hot lunch, going to the library, etc., were available to the students. The purpose of this program was to segregate the, so-called, bad and disruptive students from other students in regular school. More than thirty percent of those students dropped out of that ill-conceived program.

In 2009 the following language was contained in an executive summary prepared by Northeastern University Boston Massachusetts:

"This pipeline to prison is disproportionately filled by young black men ages 16 to 24. On any given day, nearly 23% of all young black men who have dropped out of high school, are in jail, prison, or a juvenile institute. In other words, approximately 23 of every 100 young black male dropouts, are in jail compared to only 6 to 7 of every 100 Asian, Hispanic, or white male dropouts."

I, as a black lawyer, presently see no trend that would convince me these statistics are being reversed.

My next move was to get the deposition of the two black school board members whose testimony about racism in the Charleston County School District would have been devastating. All during this litigation, the defense attorneys were saying that my clients had no case, that they were not going to pay any money to my clients, and that the school district and the other defendants participated in no discriminatory activity or conduct against my clients. I suspected that this was what they were supposed to try to drill in my head. This was not my first rodeo. And I recognized after taking the deposition of some of the defendants' witnesses, that the school district had a problem. The defense didn't have a good case. That fact became crystal clear to me when I was preparing deposition subpoenas to be served on the two black school board members so that I could take their testimony under oath. The defendants' attorney indicated he wanted to hit the pause button so that we could mediate the case before going any further. The morning of the mediation, my clients and I met at a restaurant right across the street from the school district office to discuss our strategy during the mediation. When they came into the restaurant, I noticed that they were sweating. My curiosity got the best of me. I asked why were they sweating so early in the morning. The response was they had marched around the building in which the school district headquarters is located, seven times. I surmise that they believed that the walls of Jericho were going to fall.

Mediation is a process of endurance. Each side meets jointly before the mediator to provide an opening statement and presentation of their case. The mediator then separates the two parties, usually placing them in separate rooms. The mediator then goes back and forth between the two litigants with offers and counter offers for settlement. This process goes on for an extended period of time. It is akin to survival of the fittest. My approach always in mediation, is to make the initial demand for settlement very high because it is easier to negotiate down as opposed to up. Also, the defendants will always start very low in their offer of settlement. Hopefully at the end of the six-to-eight-hour ordeal, the parties will meet somewhere in between. As usual, in this case the defendant started very low in their offer of settlement. These cases presented a unique problem. As I informed my clients before the mediation, the defendants would make cogent attempts to divide them by offering different amounts of money to settle to each of their cases. The defendants' initial offer of settlement to the plaintiffs was $2,000.00 for Ms. James, $4,000.00 for Ms. Adams and $6,000.00 for Ms. Johnson. My clients were more than prepared for this strategy by the defendants. We had discussed it on numerous occasions while eating whiting fish on my back porch. Early on, the sisterhood agreed that they would stick together, joined at the hips and would not be divided or made to turn on each other by these defendants. The initial offer was rejected with impunity. That didn't stop the defendants from continuously trying to separate these plaintiffs from each other. This tactic went on for about five hours. Each time they would make an offer of providing each plaintiff different amounts of money to settle their cases, the sisterhood stuck together. They had determined that they would be paid equally or not at all. At the end of the day, the defendants relented and paid each plaintiff a significant and equal amount of money to settle their cases. I would say that this was pretty good for cases that were repeatedly labeled by the defendants as no case at all. Because of the respect, fortitude, and unswerving commitment to the proper education of black children, in spite of the many racially-motivated obstacles put in their paths by the Charleston County School District, we still meet once every six months for lunch. I will be forever grateful to this sisterhood for, notwithstanding my initial hesitancy, allowing me to be a very minute part of that effort.

As I continued to hope for a factual situation that would be the basis for a revolutionary event to strike a deathblow against racism, my frustrations continued. In the meantime, I had to be satisfied with making very small dents into the armor guarding race discrimination. The main thrust of my rare feeling of hopelessness was that the guardrails around racism sometimes appeared to be impenetrable. It was as if I had on my shoulders four hundred years of inhumane treatment that had to be corrected. Although I would engage in every effort to, and most times did, prevail for my clients in discrimination cases, the conduct of the actors perpetrating the race discrimination would not change. This was and is especially true with governmental agencies.

As I tried to wrestle this racism monster to the ground, there were others who had the same inclination. Initially, it did not dawn on me that representing others, who could have a profound effect on the lives of young black and white children, could be a method to destroy racism. The timeframe would not be as instantaneous as I would have liked. But, outside of the hearts of men and women changing from hate, distrust, and bigotry, to love and being your fellow human being's keeper, no other avenue presented itself. That's when it became clear to me that I had an obligation, of the highest calling, to represent educators who were in the vanguard of this fight, to make real the words of the preamble to the Declaration of Independence, *"We hold these truths to be self-evident, that all men are created equal, that they are endowed by their Creator with certain unalienable rights, that among these are life, liberty, and the pursuit of happiness."* There were others who look like me who believed in those precious words despite our wretched history in this country.

One such educator was Dr. LaVerne Lebby Davis. Dr. Davis came from a family of educators. She was an original thinker. Never was she afraid of stepping outside of the box in her pursuit of inspiring and educating children. Dr. Davis in 1991, became a candidate for the principalship at St. Helena Elementary School in Beaufort County, South Carolina. The Deputy Superintendent was attempting to orchestrate a coup of naming one of his cohorts to that position, to the exclusion of Dr. Davis. The community was naturally upset because of their love for Dr. Davis. However, the one drawback was that it was powerless because of lack of parental and/or community leadership. One individual who recognized the excellent educational skills of Dr. Davis and who she knew of personally was Rev. Blake, a local black minister in a Beaufort County church. Rev. Blake was furiously interested in the proper education of all children, especially those who were black. His knowledge of her educational pedigree convinced him that she was superior at her craft. While he was not a member of the St. Helena community, nor was his church in the community, he got to know Dr. Davis because of her many visits to his place of worship. When he heard what was happening, and after speaking with Dr. Davis, Rev. Blake became upset and he uttered the words so that all could hear, including officials at the Beaufort County School District, that, "Blood would run down the streets of Beaufort if Dr. Davis is not rightfully promoted to the principalship of St. Helena Elementary School." It took a monumental effort by community and religious leaders to convince the Beaufort School District superintendent that Dr. Davis was eminently qualified to fill the vacant principal position at St. Helena Elementary School.

When she became principal, that school was rated one of two of the worst schools in Beaufort County. The superintendent expected that she would fail because of the school's history of failure. Of course, the school was predominantly black and heretofore, there was no intent on the part of the district for the pursuit of excellence at the school and there was no interest in motivating the community to make the school better. Much to the chagrin of the school district superintendent and the district, the school improved its math scores by twenty-nine percentile points within two years after Dr. Davis assumed the helm at the school. In less than four years, the school became, arguably, the best school in Beaufort County. During her tenure as principal, St. Helena Elementary School accomplished feats that no other school in Beaufort County came close to. Her math and reading scores were top in the district. The male choir called The 100 Voices began to perform all over the district and in South Carolina including the State Legislature in the State capitol. The choir was invited to perform at a museum dedication in Ghana. That's in West Africa. St. Helena began to rack up multiple awards from various state and national organizations. Students who became successful would always return and thanked her for what she instilled in them.

Our interaction began long before she became St. Helena principal. In the seventies, she was an instructor at Winthrop College, in Rock Hill, South Carolina. Later she was an employee analyst at the South Carolina Budget and Control Board before becoming an Assistant Professor at the University of South Carolina. She was eminently qualified before accepting the position of Curriculum Coordinator in the Beaufort County School District. It did not matter to her school district superiors that her innovative methods were bringing about extraordinary successes. In my many years of representing her against caustic attacks by the local school board, it became clear that they did not want my client to succeed in instilling self-confidence and cognitive educational skills in the children at her school. I'm sure that there was a significant amount of envy from her peers because of the success of the school of which she was the principal. Her desire that the students at her school become immaculately educated was infectious. All of her teachers bought into Dr. Davis' goal and vision. I dare say that administratively, St. Helena Elementary School was a well-oiled machine.

The progress of the school under her leadership, was not lost on the parents of the students and the community in general. She was given a $5,000 gift for the school by a white man from St. Helena community. The Beaufort County School District had no policy as to how a gift of this kind should be managed by the school's principal. She called the School District headquarters for guidance on how she could use the $5,000 gift to enrich the school. She was told that because there was no policy, exercise her best discretion in spending the money for the school. There was no evidence that any other school in the Beaufort County School District had received a gift of that magnitude, modest as it was, from any community person. The fact that Dr. Davis and the school had received the gift apparently angered school district officials. The School District Superintendent and Deputy Superintendent sent my client a letter telling her that she had violated School District policy in how she spent the $5,000 gift. The letter also informed her that she would be brought before the School Board for disciplinary action.

When she initially solicited my representation, immediately I deduced that this was total nonsense. There had to be a hidden motive harbored by the school superintendent for bringing a matter of this caliber before the school board. The district superintendent made its presentation to the school board concerning the alleged violation of school district policy that had been committed by Dr. Davis. Their entire effort was laughable. Our defense was that there was no policy regarding how a financial gift made to a school should be spent. And if there was such a policy, it was not in writing. We also asserted that my client sought guidance from the District superintendent's office as to how to use the $5,000 for the benefit of the school. Officials from the superintendent's office told her to use her discretion in spending those funds.

One of the board members asked, "Where is the written version of the policy Dr. Davis violated?" The superintendent responded that, "the policy is not in writing." That board member, a white female, was visibly disturbed by this baseless attempt to damage my client. Her words to the fellow board members were, "This entire hearing is a waste of our time. This is a matter that should have been handled administratively. I think the board should pay for Dr. Davis' attorney fees for this hearing." The other members of the school board did not agree to pay my attorney fees. But they unleashed a stinging verbal rebuke against both the superintendent and assistant superintendent. I was never more pleased.

Having been thoroughly embarrassed by their own feeble-minded attack on Dr. Davis, the superintendent began to engage in clandestine efforts to destroy her as a black educational administrator. We were up to the challenge. The mathematics score of the children at St. Helena Elementary School increased substantially over the first five-year period of her tenure at the school. They remained at or near the top in the entire Beaufort County School District for pretty much every year that she was the principal. One year the deputy superintendent came up with the bright idea that it was statistically impossible for these black children to have improved the math scores over such a short period of time. Presumably, he concluded that something inappropriate had occurred during the testing; after repeated audits, they never found any evidence of improper conduct by Dr. Davis or her staff during testing.

It was always very baffling to me to logically explain the disdain that the school district superintendent had against Dr. Davis. She was the epitome of what a successful principal should be. Never did she defame any of the district's leadership team to the public. If anything, she brought good notoriety to the Beaufort County School District. Her stellar work in education was recognized by the South Carolina Legislature on two separate occasions. Her arms were always open to assist other principals in the district on how to achieve the successes she had. I can fathom no reason, other than the fact that she was black and educating black children, for this constant hostility she endured from the district superintendent. Over those years, she gained the trust of the community, students, and parents. Her long work days in academically elevating St. Helena Elementary School to the top, was exceptionally appreciated by that community and parents.

Every year, the fourth grade would go to Disney World during spring break. The fifth grade would travel all over the United States and abroad. I'm not aware of any other school in Beaufort County that had that kind of community support so as to allow the students to receive that kind of exposure from traveling. There is no substitute for exposure. That is an education in and of itself.

Dr. Davis was an innovator. She was the first to introduce school uniforms to her students and parents. She introduced her children to a world beyond the county, including trips overseas to foreign countries in Africa and China. She introduced her teachers and students to the concept of the famed Algebra Project founded by Civil Rights icon Robert Mosley, along with David Dennis. She implemented a version of the Algebra Project to her staff, especially geared to elementary school children. As originally developed, the Algebra Project was designed for middle and high school children. When Dennis visited the school, he was very much impressed. He became so impressed, that his organization, Positive Innovation (which is a part of the Algebra Project), made St. Helena Elementary a focal point as well as a training site for veterans and inspiring teachers. So impressive was the Algebra Project at St. Helena Elementary, the actor Danny Glover, an Algebra Project Board member, visited Dr. Davis and the school for an entire week. For her hard work, Dr. Davis was recognized by many organizations and entities, such as the South Carolina NAACP Conference as an outstanding educator; the South Carolina Department of Education; and the South Carolina General Assembly on more than one occasion, as well as the

Congressional Black Caucus of the U.S. House of Representatives, to name a few. The district leadership, instead of building upon Dr. Davis' success, tried repeatedly to damage her personally. It was as if they were angry with her for doing what she was hired to do, educating the children. Many efforts were made through connivance to fire Dr. Davis. With each new attempt, I relished the opportunity to kick their ass one more time. In the district's pursuit to destroy Dr Davis, no scheme was too maniacal. Having failed at their many clandestine efforts to axe my client, the District Superintendent decided to use his almost absolute authority to end my client's principalship at St. Helena Elementary School.

Every school principal's contract is renewed annually. In a "right to work" state, the school district superintendent is under no obligation to renew that principal's contract. Contracts are usually signed in April for the upcoming school year. When the community found out that my client's contract would not be recommended for renewal to the school district board by the superintendent, they became outraged. Community leaders, black and white, made decisive plans to be present at the May School Board meeting. Never before had I witnessed such a well-orchestrated and concerted effort to illustrate to a local governing body that the community was not going to tolerate Dr. Davis' contract not being renewed. I appeared as her attorney at the board meeting. To my delight, the School Board's meeting room was overflowing with parents of St. Helena students, ministers, and other community leaders. There were at least 300 souls in and about a room that was designed to accommodate no more than 100 persons. The lines of parents and other interested persons meandered out and down the hallways of the School District headquarters' building. The District superintendent's plan to not renew her principal contract was stopped in its tracks. The presence of the parents and other community leaders voicing unmistakable resolute opposition to any notion of my client's contract not being renewed, caused the board to outrightly reject the superintendent's recommendation. For me as an attorney, that night was easy pickings. In sum, my total presentation to the School Board on behalf of Dr. Davis, amounted to telling its members, "Look at the community support for this black principal." It was my delight to have the opportunity to represent a client in an actual setting that was transformative. For what I saw that night transformed the St. Helena community into a power to be reckoned with by the Beaufort County School District superintendent and Board.

After that embarrassing defeat, the superintendent didn't give up in his efforts to dethrone Dr. Davis from her principalship. But all of those attempts failed miserably. She continued to serve as his principal at St. Helena Elementary School until she decided to retire.

CHAPTER 24

The VA–Edward Humes & Resto

On January 11, 1949, Ralph Henry Johnson was born in Charleston, South Carolina. After graduating from high school in 1967, he enlisted in the United States Marine Corps. Johnson, like many black Americans before him, joined the military because he loved his country. Johnson was deployed to the Republic of Vietnam in January 1968, assigned to the first reconnaissance battalion, first Marine division, as a reconnaissance scout. On March 5, 1968 while in enemy territory, Johnson's fifteen-men reconnaissance team was attacked by approximately fifty enemy soldiers. A hand grenade was thrown into the fox hole where Johnson and his fellow soldiers were trying to fend off the enemy. Unselfishly, Johnson hurled his body on the hand grenade to protect the lives of other marines. He was killed instantly. Mr. Johnson was posthumously awarded the medal of honor. On September 5, 1991, the VA Hospital in Charleston, South Carolina was renamed the Ralph H. Johnson VA Medical Center. In the lobby of the Ralph H. Johnson Medical Center is a beautiful portrait of Mr. Johnson in his full-dress Marine uniform. How ironic that this institution, a bastion of racism, displays and is named for an African-American. Mr. Johnson gave his life on foreign soil to protect his fellow white marines, yet this facility that bears his name is emblematic of racism in this country. My visits to the Ralph H. Johnson Medical Center were not to receive medical treatment. They were wholly and exclusively for the purpose of striking a blow at the facility's wide practice of racism against black employees that was unmercifully engaged in by the white executive management structure. While I have litigated numerous cases against the Ralph H. Johnson VA Medical Center in the employment discrimination context, there are two of these cases that, in my opinion, constituted the most blatant and malignant form of discriminatory practices from the facility director and other senior level managers. Discrimination based on race, runs rampant in that facility. The white management perpetrators are made to pay no personal penalty. When a monetary award is given because of a finding of discrimination, none of the responsible management officials who engaged in the discrimination suffers any repercussions. In fact, in many cases, the at fault management official is rewarded by way of promotion. Even more heinous is the fact that the same management person was allowed to continue to exhibit and practice the same kind of racially discriminatory conduct.

Perhaps the most challenging fight of my career has been the battles against the local Veterans Administration Hospital. That entity is a poster child for institutionalized race discrimination. The leadership team evolves never to include a minority or African-American. I have said, repeatedly, in depositions in the many cases that I've had against this local site, that it is a plantation. There is no conduct that the leadership would not engage in to prevent minorities from advancing, not because they are unqualified, but solely because of the hue of their epidermis.

Edward Humes was an extremely gifted electrician that worked at the VA. After being employed for more than ten years, Mr. Humes was eligible for promotion to a supervisory position in the electrical department. His supervisor, who was a Caucasian male, recommended that Mr. Humes be promoted. The facility director, a white male by the name of Dellagusa, refused to promote Mr. Humes. Perhaps a bit more background is appropriate. After Mr. Humes was not promoted, he filed a complaint with the EEOC alleging race discrimination for failure to promote. Upon going through the EEOC complaint process, a hearing before the administrative law judge was scheduled. This judge who was assigned to hear this matter was Kelly Davis. I had no previous experience with Judge Davis except that I was particularly pleased with her evenhandedness in the prehearing process. In employment discrimination cases filed with the Equal Employment Opportunity Commission the claimant can have their case tried before a single administrative judge. When I first started representing plaintiffs in these kinds of cases, I was always very leery of having a single trier of the facts and law render a decision.

At that time Mr. Humes' supervisor who recommended him for promotion, was no longer employed at the VA. He agreed to and did testify at the hearing before the administrative law judge. The most critical part of his testimony was that, although he recommended that Mr. Humes be promoted to the supervisory position, the facility director, Dellagusa, told the supervisor, "You will not promote that nigger on my watch." There were only three witnesses in this hearing. The second witness was the facility director himself. I called him as a hostile witness. In these administrative hearings, the rules of evidence are not strictly enforced. On examination,

I asked the facility director, Mr. Dellagusa, "Did you say to Mr. Humes' supervisor after he was recommended for promotion that, you will not promote that Nigger on my watch?" I truly expected that he would not answer directly or would vacillate in his answer. Much to my surprise and happiness his response was, "I may have said that." I was shocked, as was the administrative law judge. I have never before heard any supervisory official admit, in such a forthright fashion, that they made a declaration of that kind to a subordinate regarding not promoting an African-American. This man was so arrogant, yet comfortable in his pronouncement in answering my question. Although he made such an overt admission about his feelings about African-Americans, he suffered no punishment, reprimand, or admonishment. He remained the director of that facility until his tour ended. The administrative judge ordered that Mr. Humes be immediately promoted with back pay and all benefits that he would have gotten had he been justly promoted in the first instance. I would learn that the attitude of the facility director, Mr. Dellagusa, was the rule and not the exception. Others in executive positions at that facility, however, would not be as open, verbally, in regards to race discrimination as he was.

In 2005 an anonymous letter sent to the EEOC Director of that facility triggered an investigation into rampant race discrimination against black nurses. It is not the intent of this memoir to cite every discriminatory conduct that the investigatory body found to exist at the Ralph H. Johnson VA Medical Center. But I would be remiss in not revealing a few of the most glaring findings from the Administrative Board of Investigation. In the *Finding of Fact* part of the said Memorandum under the section styled *Racism*, the verbatim report states as follows:

"Through different testimony provided it is evident, and a strong perception that, white nurses are treated differently than black nurses. Some of the examples reported by the staff were scheduling practices. Through testimony there were unfair scheduling between white nurses and black nurses. White nurses were scheduled during the day shift and the black nurses were assigned the evening and night shifts. White nurses were routinely scheduled to work a different weekend that the black nurses. Inexperienced white nurses were assigned to charge nurse duties over experienced black nurses… Black Nurses assignments in addition to patient care included cleaning duties such as cleaning the refrigerator which was not part of the white nurses assignments."

Further, evidence of discriminatory conduct by Chief of Nursing Services Ms. Fraggos as set out in the report include the following:

"The allegation of Bill Hardesty, a white male nurse that practiced outside his scope of practice and that it was not reported to the State Licensing Board. It was proposed that Mr. Hardesty receive a 14 day suspension which was mitigated to a reprimand on November 13, 2003. A summary review board done on January 28, 2004 recommended that Mr. Hardesty be reported to the State Licensing Board; however the Associate Director for Patient/Nursing Services, Mary Fraggos, RN recommended on January 2, 2004 that Mr. Hardesty not be reported to the board. Ms. Fraggos' decision to not report Mr. Hardesty to the licensing board was made prior to the board making its recommendation and final report.

A black nurse found a patient's heparin drip had been turned off. Documentation in the patient's medical record revealed that she had identified the problem, notified the physician and restarted the heparin in a timely manner. A 30 day suspension was proposed for the black nurse, mitigated to a 14 day suspension and overturned by a Disciplinary Appeals Board. A white nurse by the name of Susan Hancock failed to start a heparin drip on a patient 4BN. There is no evidence that Ms. Hancock received any disciplinary action. A black nurse on 3BS failed to start a heparin drip. Due to the heparin incidents the medical center recognized the need to develop a heparin protocol in order to prevent these incidents from reoccurring in the future. This demonstrated inconsistency on how the nurse manager and the service was inconsistent on its practice for disciplinary actions and practices issues.

Monica McCrackin, a white nurse, gave a patient 14 mg. of Morphine in 1.5 hours on 4BS. This violated nursing policy, which states that a patient on the ward cannot receive more than 4mg of Morphine in a 24-hour period and did not receive any disciplinary action. A Kernig black nurse on 3BS gave a patient sublingual nitroglycerin for his chest pain. Nursing Service proposed termination on the black nurse which was mitigated to a 14 day suspension. A summary review board was requested by the medical center. Ms. Denzik took it upon herself to report the black nurse directly to the South Carolina Licensing Board and not following policy and procedure. The black nurse testified that she had been contacted by an investigator from the South Carolina State Board because she had been reported.

The black nurse was not aware that she had been reported. The black nurse was notified that the case was dismissed by the South Carolina Licensing Board. This was another example that the staff perceived of how Ms. Denzik would treat black nurses differently from white nurses. No action was taken by Ms. Fraggos."

Under the section styled *Promotions*, the following language appears:

"The board reviewed the documentation provided by the medical center on staff nurse promotions from October 2003 through June 2005. There were a total of nine promotions that had an educational waiver granted. Of the nine nurses, 88% (8) were white nurses and 12% (1) were black nurses. The board reviewed the documentation provided by the medical center on staff nurse promotions from October 2003 through June 2005. Upon reviewing the documentation the board found that during this period of time 23 (77%) were white nurses promoted and 7 (23%) were black nurses."

"The board finds through testimony that the allegations of racism are substantiated."

The primetime culprit in carrying out the systematic discriminatory scheme against African-American employees in general, and black and minority nurses in particular, was the Chief of Nursing Services Mary Fraggos. Mary Fraggos was a white female that I had deposed at least six times in employment discrimination cases against the Ralph H. Johnson VA Medical Center. She was about 5'9" and sported very short hair. She had a physique that was manly in appearance. One of my many clients from the Ralph H. Johnson VA Medical Center described Ms. Fraggos as a cross between a linebacker and a tight end. That client got no quarrel from me about the nature of her representation of the Chief of Nursing service. Notwithstanding the administrative board's finding of racism, Fraggos paid no price. Instead of Ms. Fraggos being demoted, admonished, or disciplined, she was promoted to Chief Nurse Executive of the Ralph H. Johnson VA Medical Center.

It doesn't stop there. Fraggos continued, with impunity, promoting white nurses to executive positions for which they were not qualified. One of the most glaring examples, was the promotion of a Caucasian nurse, Nicole Coxe. Ms. Coxe was blonde with Nordic features. Coxe was tall. She had light blue eyes. Arrogance was her constant companion. Truthfulness was a lacking characteristic. Some would consider her physically attractive. From my perspective, beauty begins on the inside. It is being fair, caring, and having a compassion to do what is right. Internal beauty has no components that resemble lying and extraordinary self-importance. Against those measuring sticks, she was not pretty.

In the federal government, an opening for a position that needs to be filled is advertised on the USA Job website with a vacancy announcement. Each vacancy announcement has a minimum of six numbers that identifies that announcement. Those numbers must be placed in a designated block on the applicant's application. Among other things on the advertisement, there is a date, normally two weeks, in which all applications for the position must be submitted. It is mandatory that all applications be signed by the applicant. Applications that are not signed by the applicant are incomplete and must be rejected. Applications are graded by a panel. That panel determines, from the applications, who are the best qualified candidates for the position. Interviews are held by the panel members for the three best qualified candidates for the vacant position.

The client that I represented, Milagros Resto, who was a minority, followed these mandatory requirements to the letter.

The government can, at any time, rescind the vacancy announcement and not fill the position. Once the vacancy announcement is rescinded, there can be no hiring of any one for the position under the rescinded vacancy announcement. Some two weeks after the vacancy announcement was closed, Mary Fraggos re-opened the vacancy announcement for one day, so that her girl, Nicole Coxe, the blonde, could apply. The application that was submitted by or on behalf of Ms. Coxe was unsigned, had no vacancy announcement number on it, and it was for a position that she had applied for two years earlier.

As Coxe walked into the conference room to be deposed, she displayed a demeanor of white privilege. Her aura cast off the attitude of *how dare you black sons of bitches* question me about being promoted to the position of nurse executive? I am entitled because I am white. Being offended by her body language, I made a conscious decision to embark upon a line of questions that would break her prejudice ass down. My thoughts were clear. This white woman had to be informed, through brutal questioning, that she would pay a price.

During the deposition, my strategy has always been to be as brutal with the main perpetrator as possible. Inflict emotionally monumental pain through a thousand cuts. The more savage the questions, the quicker this villain realizes that she had no position of superiority to me or my client because we were minorities. I reasoned that she would be more disgruntled because of the fact that these questions would be coming from a black man. For that two and a half hours, her world of white entitlement would crumble. She had no choice. She would have to answer all of my questions under oath.

Through crushing questions, Coxe's answers put her in a box. She insisted that she submitted two applications. As I thought, she would have to acknowledge that the application that was produced by her agency to me was unsigned and for a position that she applied for some two years earlier. Her testimony was that there was another signed application that was sent to USA Jobs. The government provided for me a plethora of documents that supposedly contained this phantom application. I gave her all of those documents and said, "I want you to find the application that you said is more current that you submitted." Before she could answer, the government's attorney interjected, "Oh, it's not in there. I can tell you that."

That admission by her attorney was not enough for me. Through more penetrating and exacting questions, she admitted that she had no acknowledgment from USA Jobs that she sent this phantom application to them.

Q: "Do you have any proof other than what you're telling us here today that there was an acknowledgment letter regarding that other application?"

A: "Not in my possession."

She further admitted that neither one of the applications, including the phantom one, was signed by her.

In her deposition, Ms. Fraggos said:

Q: "According to your testimony, that application is unsigned, and according to your previous testimony should have been returned to Ms. Coxe?"

A: "Correct."

A: "…And now that I think about it, I don't think they give us the applications."

Fraggos admitted in her deposition that Coxe violated VA rules in the unsigned application that was for a vacancy position advertised some eighteen months earlier. Consider the following testimony from Fraggos:

Q: "In submitting this application, she violated the V.A. directives; has she not?"

A: "Yes, sir."

Q: "So if that is the case, Ms. Coxe really never applied for this job?"

A: "I would assume that she had an incomplete application that was invalid."

My client, Mrs. Resto, scored higher than anyone on the assessment by the review panel. The second highest score from the review panel belonged to an African-American female. The two highest scores belong to minority applicants. Nicole Coxe, without a proper application for the position, was selected by Mary Fraggos to fill the opening. My client raised hell, so much so, that the vacancy announcement was then rescinded. That meant that no one would be selected for the Nurse Executive position, but Ms. Fraggos was determined to give the position to her blonde beauty, Nicole Coxe. She caused a new vacancy announcement to be issued for the same Nurse Executive position. All applicants for the position had to apply by December 9, 2014. My client reapplied for the Nurse Executive position under the new vacancy announcement. Ms. Coxe did not. Mary Fraggos selected Nicole Coxe for the position on December 8, 2014, under the same vacancy announcement that had been previously canceled by the government. Under the cancelled vacancy announcement, Ms. Coxe had the third highest score. Determining to extract a pound of flesh from Fraggos, I posed the following questions to her during her deposition.

> Q: "So again my question to you is: Explain to me, if you can, how you announced that Nicole Coxe was selected under a canceled vacancy announcement number."

> A: "I can't explain that."

My soul cried out, in a nonverbal fashion, *"It's called racism, imbecile, practiced by you."* Fraggos, from 2010 through June 13, 2016, hired only white persons for positions where she was the selecting official.

> Q: "So read Number 19 for me."

The government admitted that,

> A: "In reference to the two previous interrogatories, over the past ten years—over the last ten years state the number of times a Caucasian person has been selected to fill a position where Ms. Fraggos was the selecting official. "Since 2010 only persons who appear to be Caucasian[s] have been selected by Ms. Fraggos."

Other senior level executives (in cahoots with Ms. Fraggos) participated in practicing systemic racism against minority employees at the Ralph H. Johnson VA Medical Center.

How Nicole Coxe was promoted to the nurse executive position without having filled out a mandatory application, she responded, "I guess she shouldn't have been selected." In my mind, I said, "Moron you selected her!" I found that astounding because Ms. Fraggos was the selecting official. To try and cover her tracks, Ms. Fraggos convened what was called the PENTAD. That, as she explained it, was senior-level executive officials who are used to select nurse executives. Fraggos claimed that written statements by these senior level executives were used in her decision to promote Nicole Coxe to Nurse Executive. Of course, they were all white women or men. They weaved a tangled web in which they got caught. All of the PENTAD members that gave the blessings, in written statements, to the promotion of Nicole Coxe, dated their writings three to ten weeks after Coxe was promoted. Rhetorically, I asked, how could Fraggos rely on these statements to promote Coxe. Given my litigation against this VA, their conduct, in this instance, is not surprising. My client was handsomely paid for not being promoted. However, Ms. Coxe is still in the position for which she did not apply.

CHAPTER 25

Tracey Washington

On June 5, 2014, I was on my way to a hearing, rehearsing to myself the arguments that I would present to the trial judge in a criminal matter. My cell phone rang. Glancing down to look at the phone, a number appeared that I was not familiar with. I initially thought that this was simply another spam call. Normally, I do not answer my cell phone when there is an unfamiliar number calling. But I thought, what the heck, answer the cell phone. I did. The voice of a female said, "Good morning, my name is Tracey Washington. Is this Attorney Edward Brown?" In a rather cavalier fashion, I said, "That's what they tell me." I had no idea who Tracey Washington was or why she was calling me at 11 o'clock in the morning. Still being rather nonchalant, I said, "To what do I owe the pleasure of this call?" After a brief moment of idle chat, Ms. Washington said she was referred to me by a previous client whom I had represented against the United States Department of Veterans Affairs. My interest peaked, in that I was interested to know first, who was the former client. She provided me with the name and said that, "I understand that you are called the David against the Goliath Department of Veterans Affairs." I've never been able to comfortably accept compliments. In my normal self-deprecating fashion, I responded, "I've heard that rumor." I've never thought of myself as being anything other than a black professional who worked very hard to prepare his cases against the adversary. I've often said to others who have made similar comments, that being a good lawyer is like playing competitive golf. You don't have to be the best golfer. You just have to be better than the golfers that you are competing against on that day.

With a limited amount of time before the hearing in the criminal matter to which I was headed began, I asked Ms. Washington what the issue was that she was having with the Department of Veterans Affairs. In a nutshell, she said that she had been discriminated against by the VA because of her race. I asked if she would call me at two o'clock eastern standard time. Ms. Washington was calling me from the West Coast. After my hearing in the criminal matter, I began to ponder why would someone from the West Coast call me to represent them in an adversarial matter against the Department of Veterans Administration on the West Coast. I didn't believe that I would be interested in a cross-country representation, to the extent that if this matter had to be filed in Federal Court, that would have to occur on the West Coast. Given the ferocity with which the Department of Veterans Affairs sometimes defends discrimination cases, I thought it would probably be best for me to give Ms. Washington some advice and encourage her to hire a lawyer in that area of the country. It dawned on me that perhaps I ought to listen to Ms. Washington's account of what she believed the facts to be that constituted the discriminatory conduct by the VA.

At two o'clock, Ms. Washington called. I was curious as to how she got my cell phone number. I was informed by Ms. Washington that she insisted that my previous client give her my cell phone and office numbers.

She stated that in 2012, she settled a race discrimination case against the VA for $75,000. A part of the settlement agreement was that she would not apply for employment with any other VA facility in the region where that Veterans Administration hospital was located. In terms of the Veterans Administration, the United States is divided into approximately eighteen Veterans Integrated Service Networks. They are commonly referred to as VISN. The settlement agreement forbids Ms. Washington from applying for a position with a VA facility in that Veterans Service Network. The agreement however, did not prevent Ms. Washington from being employed by the VA in other Veterans Integrated Service Networks in the United States. The settlement agreement resolved two pending race discrimination cases that Ms. Washington had before the Equal Employment Opportunity Commission and the Merit System Protection Board. Her personnel file, as the settlement agreement provided, would reflect that she voluntarily resigned from her position at the North Carolina VA facility.

After resigning, Ms. Washington immediately began to file applications with other VA facilities in other regions of the country for employment. Over the next two-years, she filed a total of forty-two applications. Each time she was refused employment. Generally, when an opening occurs at a VA facility, a panel is appointed to assess the applicants that are best qualified to interview for the position. A part of that assessment process is a review by the panel of the applicant's personnel folder. Federal agencies, such as the VA, refer to this folder as the OEF file. That panel usually compiles a best qualified list of three applicants. Generally, those candidates are then interviewed by the panel. The panel then makes a recommendation as to who the selecting official should hire from among those candidates. Ms. Washington was always on the best qualified list, but got only one interview. She was informed by the HR Director of the West Coast VA Hospital that they wanted to hire her, but that her Official Personnel Folder (OPF) revealed that she resigned from her previous position with the North Carolina VA in lieu of being terminated. In federal employment parlance that categorization is a death knell. Very rarely, if ever, will a black employee be hired by a federal agency if that employee was allowed to resign in lieu of removal.

That classification lodged in Ms. Washington's personnel folder was remarkably erroneous. The agreement executed by Ms. Washington and the Director of the North Carolina VA Medical Center clearly created a contract between the two parties. After viewing the agreement, I determined that the VA had set up a potential legal minefield for Ms. Washington.

The Merit System Protection Board approved the agreement between Ms. Washington and the North Carolina Veterans Medical Center. I hypothesized that the government would argue that any breach of this agreement by the North Carolina Veterans Medical Center would have to be resolved by the Merit System Protection Board. Generally, the Merit System Protection Board can correct personnel records and, in very limited instances, award monetary damages for race discrimination. The breach of an agreement of this caliber was not a matter over which the Merit System Protection Board has jurisdiction. My analysis was that the North Carolina Veterans Medical Center entered into an agreement with Ms. Washington. Ms. Washington kept her end of the agreement. The government did not. The course with the most obstacles for Ms. Washington would have been to proceed before the Merit System Protection Board. I was determined not to enter into that legal nightmare. The Merit System Protection Board is a very obtuse agency. Although they can entertain a discrimination claim, it is fraught with procedural traps. I realized that the VA's attorneys would prefer that path.

After some cursory analysis, it became clear to me that this case could be pursued directly against the VA for breach of the contract or agreement that it made with Ms. Washington. A citizen cannot sue the government without the permission of the sovereign to be sued. The avenue to bring a breach of contract action against the Department of Veterans Affairs was the Tucker Act. Under the Tucker Act, the United States waived its sovereign immunity to certain kinds of claims. Although the government is immune from lawsuits as a general rule, the Tucker Act specifically permits breach of contract claims against the federal government. Also, to attain a full monetary redress for her breach of contract claim, the Tucker Act was the legal vehicle that needed to be driven. I filed a lawsuit for breach of contract, on behalf of Ms. Washington against the United States in the United States Court of Federal Claims. I knew that the government would file a motion with the court to dismiss this lawsuit on the grounds that this matter was within the exclusive jurisdiction of the Merit System Protection Board. I felt confident that this motion would fail because of the overwhelming evidence that the North Carolina Veterans Medical Center had breached its agreement with Ms. Washington. Although the agreement between Ms. Washington and the North Carolina Veterans Medical Center allowed my client to voluntarily resign from the VA, the VA put in Ms. Washington's personnel file, *"Resignation in lieu of removal: Within a reasonable period of time not to exceed forty five (45) days of this fully executed Agreement, the Agency will take all necessary action to substitute Appellant's*

Removal for a voluntary resignation effective 1 December 2011. The change to resignation shall be made in Appellant's eOFP and on any paper documents wherever they may be located."

There was nothing extraordinarily complicated in the settlement agreement that the North Carolina Veterans Medical Care Center made with Ms. Washington. That facility was trying to terminate her because she had filed a discrimination complaint. And as she had every right to do, she stood up. When they agreed, Ms. Washington and the facility, to part ways, she was paid $75,000 and allowed to resign. This kind of agreement is reached routinely between federal agencies and employees that agencies want to get rid of. Ms. Washington in ascertaining this settlement, had defeated the discriminatory racial instincts of her supervisor, a white male. Thus, it was always mind boggling to me why her supervisor would approve the language to be put in her personnel file which indicated that she was allowed to resign in lieu of being removed. That was not a genius moment. The white supervisor had to believe that Ms. Washington would not discover that written communication in her personnel file. And for two years he was correct.

However, when it was brought to Ms. Washington's attention that this negative indication was in her personnel file, she immediately emailed the Human Resources Department at the North Carolina Veterans Medical Care Center. The HR Director sent an email to my client admitting that the language that was in Ms. Washington's personnel file should not have been there, and that they would engage in efforts to try to remove it. The icing on the cake was a phrase in the email from the HR Director which said, *"I apologize for any inconvenience this may have caused you."* We had the proverbial smoking gun. Even with this evidence, the VA still did not want to voluntarily compensate Ms. Washington for not being able to secure another job at a different Veterans Integrated Service Networks facility. They had breached the agreement made with Ms. Washington and I was determined that she would be adequately compensated.

After filing the lawsuit in the United States Court of Claims, the VA insisted that they were only obligated to fix the language in Ms. Washington's personnel file. It was as if no one cared that my client had suffered for two years, in that she could not attain any meaningful employment. The attorney representing the government was a young Caucasian female based in the United States Department of Justice Office in Washington, DC. Most of our telephonic communications during this litigation were cordial and reasonable. However, her job was to defeat my client's claim of breach of contract. Despite the affable demeanor she displayed over the telephone, I knew she had every resource that the Department of Justice could muster to defend the VA's position. Given the facts of this case, I firmly believe that if my client and I got by the Motion to Dismiss, which the government was sure to file, we would prevail. But I still knew that to get to that point would take somewhat of a monumental effort on our part.

In that vein, I researched every case that had similar or liked facts to Ms. Washington's case. I didn't find a case that was exactly like this one, but what I found was close enough. I filed with the court, a well-reasoned response, with extensive case law citations, Memorandum of Law in opposition to the Veterans Administration's Motion to Dismiss Ms. Washington's breach of contract claim. A short period of time thereafter, the Court of Claims issued an order denying the Government's Motion to Dismiss my client's claim. As I thought, the government came to the table with their negotiating hats on. After an extensive period of back and forth offers and counter offers for settlement, the case was concluded for a healthy six-figure amount. Ms. Washington's white male supervisor at the North Carolina VA Medical Center suffered no consequences. I believe that is called *white privilege*. Because of this man's racial proclivities, the government had to compensate my client with a substantial amount of money.

Interestingly enough, I never personally met with Ms. Washington; we video chatted. About six months after her case was concluded, she referred another client to me. That client was located in the southwestern United States. Much to my surprise, when we initially talked, her opening words to me were, "Are you Ed Brown the VA killer?" My response was, "I've heard that rumor."

CHAPTER 26

Charles Lockemy

Some may have developed a thought that I have an unapologetic dislike for white people. To that charge, if it is peripherally in anyone's mind, I plead not guilty. I will admit that I am, with every fiber of my being, irretrievably opposed to that which is not right, just, or equitable. For me, in part, that means that I will always be against engaging in nefarious conduct against another human being because of their race. The color of one's skin cannot and should never be used as a factor in determining the worth or character of the person.

Charles Lockemy was a patriot. After retiring from the military, he became a private detective. I met Charles after a hearing in a divorce case. When he initially approached me, I was very skeptical about his motives to the extent that we were on opposite sides in the divorce matter. We exchanged professional cards. About two weeks later, Charles called me and asked if I would represent a woman who wanted a divorce from her spouse because her husband was having an affair with other women that lived in their neighborhood. I didn't know whether this client of Charles' was white, but I strongly suspected that. Up to that point in my practice, I had never represented a white woman in a divorce proceeding. I somewhat hesitantly agreed to meet with Charles' client at my office. I was surprised that Charles Lockemy brought his client to my office for the initial interview. During the back and forth of the interview, Charles Lockemy extolled my worth as a lawyer. Never before and not since, has anyone heaped professional praise on me in the presence of another as Charles Lockemy did that day. I was astonishingly surprised. Here was a white man whom I didn't know, but he convinced his female client that there was no better lawyer to represent her in this divorce action. The most astounding locution that came from his mouth was that because of how good I was as a lawyer, she would need a fifteen thousand dollars ($15,000.00) deposit to retain my services. I was truly amazed. Before that case, I had never received the deposit in a divorce case from anyone of more than $5,000.00. Charles' client, after signing a retainer's contract, wrote me a check for $15,000.

Because of the evidence that Charles had secured proving that the husband was committing adultery with a neighbor, an award was made of attorney fees in the amount of $25,000 that was paid by the cheating husband for my services in representing his wife. At some point before the end of this divorce case, I asked Charles why he wanted me to represent this white woman in that divorce proceeding. He said, "I've heard great things about you as a lawyer and I think you do not know your worth given the results that you get when professionally representing your clients." From that time forward, every client Charles Lockemy referred to me, professionally, would bring a substantial check or cash as a deposit. The minimum that I ever received from any of his referrals was $7,500. Usually, the evidence of the spouse cheating was so convincing that my client always came out on the winning end. Not one time, over the many years that I knew him, did he ever ask me for a kickback from the fees that I collected from the client or the cheating spouse.

My relationship with Charles Lockemy taught me a valuable lesson, one that I would never forget and I used going forward in my professional career. Never undervalue the services that you render to your clients and never let anyone else diminish the value, monetarily, of your professional skill set. Charles Lockemy was a good person. Over the years of our friendship, we developed a special affinity for one another. He never had a crossword for me, nor I for him. It was as if he were specially sent to encourage me, support me, and make me understand, to use his words, *how good I was as a lawyer.* While I am not so sure that my professional skills were so extraordinary, I do know that every time I entered into an adversarial proceeding, especially where losing would be to let injustice prevail, I had to win. In that effort, I was determined to use all oratorical and legal skills necessary to vindicate the rights of my client. The ultimate honor was bestowed upon me by Charles Lockemy's family at his funeral. I was asked by his wife to sit with the family.

This concludes volume one. However, the stories that I must tell do not end here. There is much more to come.

Acknowledgements

On June 11, 1982, I embarked upon the journey of becoming a solo practitioner. With me at the beginning of that path was a person that became, a friend, a paralegal, a sounding board, and everything that contained the ingredients for a successful law practice. One of my clients once said Debbie Robinson was marginally slight in stature. I immediately responded that his observations were unimportant to me. What was important is I, with unabashed zeal, said that she was unparalleled in intellect. Never before in my time on this earth, have I met a human being as gifted as Debbie. Some have said that I am not all that I could have been. To that I would reply, while that might be true, all that I am I owe, in monumental measures, to my secretary Debbie Robinson. After a period of time, the professional unison between us was so finely tuned such that I could start a sentence while leaving the room and she would finish the thought, sentence, or paragraph with surgical precision.

Her loyalty is something to behold. What went on in my law practice was more secured than the gold in Fort Knox, Kentucky. Never once in our thirty-nine years have there been a cross exchange between us. There were times when I'm sure she sensed that I thought that the adversary we faced was overwhelming. But always at the right moment she would say we'll get this done. Those words created in me a level of comfort that we would and more than eighty-five percent of the time prevail. A case in point. I filed a lawsuit against a major marine shipping company. They had a total of six lawyers. They were at a disadvantage because I had Debbie. We answered with clarity and persuadeness, every pleading, motion, etc. that they filed. At the end of the day, we prevailed. That was usual. It was abnormal, and rare, when we did not win by way of settlement or court proceeding. To her, my trusted comrade in battle, I say thank you from the bottom of my heart.

Over forty years ago, I met Hugh Kyler Davis, Esquire. For a brief period of time (1980–1982), we practiced law together. Over the years, our friendship was strengthened by the war stories that we, from time to time, shared about our focused endeavor to seek that elusive result call justice for our clients. We would compare notes, develop trial strategy and refined to oral argument to be presented at trials or motion hearings. More often than not, we had to climb the rough side of the mountain to get to its top to achieve a degree of success. Others did not have that burden. I firmly believe those tribulations made us better lawyers and human beings. To this day, I am forever grateful for the camaraderie I enjoy with my friend and I thank him for the many hours he put in my efforts to put pen to paper in constructing this memoir. He was always encouraging and not once did he ever say no when I sought his advice and help. Mr. Davis has been and continues to be a true legal warrior in this seemingly never-ending battle for justice and equality for black and poor people.

About the Author

The youngest of ten children, Edward M. Brown was born and reared on one of the barrier islands off the coast of South Carolina. In 1967 he graduated from St. John's High School in Johns Island, South Carolina.

After attending Bishop College in Dallas, Texas for two years, he received a Crown-Zellerbach Fellowship to attend and study at the University of California at Berkeley. With a major in political science and a minor in economics, he graduated from Berkeley with a bachelor's degree in 1971. After a very brief period in the corporate world, Mr. Brown received a Ford Foundation fellowship to attend Thurgood Marshall School of Law at Texas Southern University in Houston, Texas. In 1982 he became a solo practitioner in Charleston, South Carolina. During his entire forty-two years, he maintained an active practice in constitutional law, employment discrimination law, Civil Rights Law, criminal law as well as other areas of the practice of law.

Connect

If you enjoyed this book, leave a review on Amazon.com, and please purchase copies for those who can benefit. Visit the author online at http://edwardbrownesq.com/.

www.ingramcontent.com/pod-product-compliance
Lightning Source LLC
Chambersburg PA
CBHW072307210326
41519CB00057B/3051